Living on the Roof of the World

Compiled by Jin Zhiguo

NEW WORLD PRESS

First Edition 2011

Compiled by Jin Zhiguo
Translated by Transn
Edited by Li Shujuan
Cover Design by Qing Qing Chong Studio

ISBN 978-7-5104-1414-5

Published by
NEW WORLD PRESS
24 Baiwanzhuang Street, Beijing 100037, China

Distributed by
NEW WORLD PRESS
24 Baiwanzhuang Street, Beijing 100037, China
Tel: 86-10-68995968
Fax: 86-10-68998705
Website: www.newworld-press.com
E-mail: frank@nwp.com.cn

Printed in the People's Republic of China

Living
on the Roof
of the
World

Compiled by Jin Zhiguo

NEW WORLD PRESS

CONTENTS

No. 1 Rock Band of the Tibetan Plateau

By Deqing Baizhen

All of a sudden, rock music can be heard from street to street in Lhasa, adding a special and fresh flavor to the city. Five years ago Tenzin Dawa established the Unplugged, Tibet's first folk-rock music club, and ever since a new sound, Tibetan folk with rock 'n' roll, has been tantalizing audiences, passers-by and the neighborhood. Now his band, Celestial Baton, has released their first CD and it is everywhere in Lhasa, changing the way Tibetans think about their music.

Tashi Phuntsok, who plays bass, is the leader of Celestial Baton. Tenzin Dawa is the drummer, and the heart and soul of the band. Sonam Tenzin plays lead guitar and Sonam Nima, rhythm guitar. Sonam Nianza is the lead singer. The band began to play together a few years ago. They decided to burn a CD when they saw that their music had begun to stir up a deepening response from their audiences.

A celestial baton, according to Tibetan Buddhism, is a powerful rod that can repel evil and so symbolizes the value of Tibetan culture. It means, "to be a thunderbolt," explains Tenzin Dawa. "The name also captures our high-pitched, soul-penetrating music. Our Tibetan music creates a dialogue with the more universal expression of life which is at the heart of rock 'n' roll. We want to reflect the truth and beauty in our society and, together with rock, reveal the goodness of human nature."

Their Music

Though their music is very strikingly new, they are very attentive, deliberate and thoughtful when they write the music and lyrics to their songs. Songs such as *Desire*, *Rinzin Wangmo*, and *Labudabu* are based on original folk songs. The purpose of these folk songs was always to teach the values of goodness and beauty, and the band is careful to capture this in their new and distinctive renditions as well.

Labudabu, for example, is a well-known imaginary figure, who in fables takes his father's place in the army. However, the band changed this. For them Labudabu is an unambitious man who leads a meaningless and unexciting life. He gets lost in daydreams of success and fortune. The song is scathingly sarcastic, because Labudabu has clearly lost his sense of good and beauty. With a hip-hop beat, the band turns the song into a funny teasing reminder of what is important in life. Sonam Nima explains: "I feel that the hip-hop beat here is extremely mind-blowing. The old version of the song makes it difficult for people today to learn how to really deal with their lives. If we use the old ideas, the slow rhythm, then the song doesn't get where we need it to go. This way it works just right."

In terms of style, *Labudabu* starts out rhythmically like a Tibetan nursery rhyme. The popular hip-hop beat is in the refrain. It gives a totally new impression to people when they hear it, and at the same time, they are caught in an inexplicable sense of *déjà vu*."

Amaqiangmala (meaning Song of the Highland Barley Wine) is a very old folk song. The band borrowed from this famous Tibetan toast song and turned it into rap music. It is the first time that songs in Tibetan have been rapped. Sonam Nima says that this folk song has been sung for centuries with the same old tune. They wanted to put in something new and so added a touch of Western forms and rhythms. "Now it sounds really good and the song has come alive," he says.

They wrote the first song in Tibetan to help preserve the Tibetan antelopes from poaching. Again, Tashi Phuntsok: "We have a Tibetan hero, Suonandajie, who died trying to save them. We are singers, so we cannot catch those poachers as much as we would like to do so. Writing a song for our antelopes is our way of helping them. We humbly offer this as our gift to them."

The band has added traditional instruments not usually played together and it is marvelous. The traditional dramyin, for example, is a lute instrument with six strings and usually played as an accompaniment for Buddhist songs. In their CD it has a special role throughout the whole album, interweaving the evoking sounds of the ancient plateau into the music. "Many ethnic instruments can also play modern music. It is only the shackles on the minds of people that stop us. If you break free from the idea that traditional musical instruments can only be for traditional music, you will see something much more fascinating and brilliant," Tashi Phuntsok comments.

Bian Luo, a noted Tibetan songwriter and lyricist, spoke highly of the album: "Celestial Baton has made a great contribution to Tibetan music. First, they have added their own interpretation of history in the form of rock 'n' roll. As to the music itself, the introduction of such new language in Tibetan music is bold and successful. The biggest breakthrough, however, is the strong empathy shown in their songs and their straightforward lyrics."

Tradition and Finding a Way Forward Together

Of course, criticism has also arisen. Some say that they are defiling folk songs with their new interpretations. The band, however, faces these concerns with equanimity and emphasizes that their music is but the expression of their artistic feelings: "Others may feel our music a mockery of folk songs, but this is only their particular understanding and views. The song, *Amaqiangmala*, for example, was once popular but was mostly unknown to most young people until we reintroduced it with our adaptation. Now the song can be heard in many places. It's our contribution. From our viewpoint, we think we are carrying our ethnic music forward," explains Tashi Phuntsok,

Music should connect with people and help them face social problems squarely. This way they can realize what they need to do. Facing the doubts from the musicians who play traditional music, he insists: "Despite variations, a folk song will always be itself in nature. Just like people, you may wear whatever you desire, but the belief and soul in you will never change so easily with what is fashionable."

Growing in the Soil of Traditional Music

Their musical creativity has not stopped. The band is now looking for inspirations in other areas of the rich Tibetan musical landscape, namely pastoral songs that resound on the grasslands and also work songs.

They consider every inch of the inspiring land of Tibet to be an unfailing source of creativity. "We have an inexhaustible supply for our music. You may hear a different tone passing by one mountain for example to the next. The lead chanter in a Buddhist temple often has a deep, rich and resonant bass voice, which we'd also like to capture as well. At the same time our music can

be brought to life by looking from a different perspective. We listened very carefully to the normal 'Da-a-ga Song,' an antiphonal song with varied rhythms between a man and a woman and we found we could make it even better with our instrumental accompaniment and rhythms. Rap can be added to Tibetan operas as well," observes Sonam Nianza.

In early 1990s, musicians in Tibet tried rock 'n' roll but they didn't know much about the culture and traditions of Western music and Tibet was not ready to hear it then. Now, for this new generation, Celestial Baton is able to combine traditional folk music with this outside influence. Listening to both since their childhood the members of the band are able to integrate them. Giving full range to the ethnic elements as well as broadening the rock with forms of hip-hop, rap, R&B and blues, they've created their own brand of music.

All of the members of the band have daytime jobs. Tashi Phuntsok gave up his well-paid job in telecommunications and switched to a five-year study of music in Tibet University. He is presently a teacher of music in a secondary school. Tenzin Dawa runs the Unplugged. The lead singer Sonam Tenzin is a dancer with the Singing and Dancing Troupe of Tibet Autonomous Region. Sonam Nianza, the lead guitarist, is a German-speaking tour guide. Sonam Nima, the rhythm guitarist, is an auditor.

Other such groups who have spearheaded such ideas are Cui Jian, the first rocker in China, who used *suona* (double-reed wind instrument with a flaring metal bell) and zither (*guzheng*, a 16-26 stringed zither with movable bridges) in rock music in the 1980s, and Askar, the rock band in Xinjiang, who successfully brings tamboura into their music.

Songwriter Bian thinks that untrained individuals bring fresh perspectives to music. "Professionals may see only the simple orchestration and melody in this music, but it is just these unsophisticated techniques that are the highlights."

Celestial Baton permits innovative dialogue to occur to Tibetans and their music. The band brings new vigor to Tibetan music and its culture as well. Tibetan rock music can now take its place in the international history of music and enrich world culture. At the same time, the music of Tibet will now continue to evolve into the future.

Lobsang Tenzin and the Legendary Tibetan Medical Family of Qiemo

By Jin Zhiguo

Just like all cultural phenomena in Tibet traditions have an aura of mysticism. Tibetan medicine, with its 2,000-year-old history, profound cultural presence, myriad of stories and legends, unique medical ideas and means of treatment, has intrigued people around the world.

If you want to know about Tibetan medicine and pharmacology, you need to know about Lobsang Tenzin, a Tibetan doctor who is regarded as one of the best doctors today.

He comes from a family which has produced several great physicians during the past centuries. And, like his ancestors, he uses new ideas as well as the family's colossal medical library when curing his patients. His method combines Tibetan medicine, traditional Chinese medicine and Western medicine and has resolved lots of complicated cases.

His reputation has gradually spread from Tibetan-inhabited areas to central China and then into the world. Tibetan medication is attracting more and more patients. If they are not able to visit Tibet, they ask friends and relatives to bring back medicine that he has prescribed.

7

Today the humanity and ideas behind Tibetan medical concepts of diagnosis has aroused keen interest and research has begun into this unique medicine and pharmacology. The concept of the human being is different from that of Western medicine, or traditional Chinese medicinal sciences. Its distinctive analysis of the human body includes the bonds between the patient, family and the doctor. Finally there are ethical principles the patients must follow that are prescribed by Tibetan medicine.

Finally, the reverence for the doctor is also a feature of Tibetan medicine and pharmacology. There are also complicated processes of preparing drugs. There are sacred blessings and prayers for every procedure. Even meticulous procedures to make pills which are wrapped in red silk or yellow satin, look somehow holy and sacred.

The Family from Aga

Lobsang Tenzin's ancestral home is in Aga, Gonjo County, Chamdo Prefecture in eastern Tibet. It is a beautiful town surrounded by high mountains and deep valleys. Virgin forests cover the land so it is spectacular in winter and colorful in summer.

The busy turning of seasons doesn't ripple the tranquility of his family. It is free of disturbances from the outside world. As a result, life here is simple and slow, making people's live a long life. Most of the families, from generation to generation, live the way of their ancestors.

Only a few people walk out of the mountains, bathing in the sunshine and breathing the air of the outside world. There is always someone from Lobsang Tenzin's family among these people. Their reputation comes from cultivating superb medical skills, a lineage of living Buddhas and magistrates, as well as a spirit of adventure and seeking personal cultivation.

Lobsang Tenzin's great-grandfather learned medical skills from his father when he was young. Then, when he was 30, he traveled to India, Nepal and Sikkim as a roving doctor. He spent many years and all his youth in exotic places. He visited famous doctors, collecting rare herbs adding to the precious medical fortune of the Qiemo family.

When he returned home, he was a 60-year-old man. He brought with him numerous medical books, medicines and apparatus for which he needed more than 30 horses to carry home.

Lobsang Tenzin's grandfather was a baby when his father left. He only really met his father as an adult. Before that, he relied on the medical skills of the family for his training and practising.

When his father returned, he told his son many anecdotes about the outside world. He especially explained the medical concepts that were different from traditional Tibetan medicine, such as bloodletting therapy, smoke therapy, pointing therapy, massage and rubbing therapy.

Like father, like son. All these stories inspired the 30-year-old son, who wished to be like his father and go out into the world. His father approved and made a rough itinerary for him. Carrying just simple medical equipment, he started on his journey.

He not only went to Sikkim, India, Nepal and other places his father had been to, but also to Medog to check the medicinal materials there, to Nayu of Mainling (this was said to be the source of medicine of the founder of Tibetan medicine, Yotok Yonten Kongpo), and to Wutai Mountain in Shanxi Province. He spent 26 years traveling, almost as long as his father's journey. Like his father, he brought back numerous books on medicine.

From then on, the family introduced traditional Chinese medicine into their medical skills. We can assume that during the 26 years of travel of Lobsang Tenzin's grandfather, he spent much of the time and energy on natural medicine. The journey for medical practice, study and research did not only enrich the medical wealth of the Qiemo family, but also brought in many unknown plants. While he led the family, they enjoyed an unprecedentedly high reputation in the medical field. Their fame spread from Chamdo to Lhasa.

Lobsang Tenzin's grandfather lived 103 years. In his last years, the society was under tremendous change. For safety, the old man put many medical books and materials in caves or donated them to monasteries. He wrote prescriptions for various diseases and handed 360 secret prescriptions down to his third son, who is Lobsang Tenzin's father.

Working as a roving doctor became a tradition. Lobsang Tenzin's father left home at the age of 18. The next year, a young lady from a rich family, his childhood playmate, found him in Mainling, and married him. The lady became Lobsang Tenzin's mother. The young couple went south to Medog.

Lobsang Tenzin explained why so many doctors in the family went to Medog. Tibetan medicine and pharmacology has three schools, one relies on plants for medicine, another on minerals, and the other on the bones and flesh of animals. The Qiemo family is from the first school. The proportion of medicine the Qiemo family prepares is 10 percent minerals, 20 percent bones and flesh of animals and 70 percent plants. Most of the medicinal plants only grow in Medog.

Perhaps it was a coincidence that in the perpetual spring of Medog, which is also called "Pema Gang" (Lotus Mountain), a new successor of the family was conceived. Like the births of other living Buddhas and legendary men, the birth and childhood of Lobsang Tenzin had its own legendary omens.

After his mother became pregnant in Medog, the couple began the nine-month journey home. On their way they stopped in Ninga Village of Mainling County. On the morning of September 15, 1944, the sun did not rise and the village was quiet. A storm of hailstones suddenly rained down. A few minutes later, the hailstones stopped. Villagers were afraid that their crops were ruined and rushed out to check them.

To their astonishment, the hailstones were not white but full of different colors. Even more peculiar, the hailstones didn't fall on the fields, just on the ground around the houses. While the villagers were still in confusion, a strong beam of sunlight burst out from the dark sky and clouds turned to golden red. A rainbow spanned the sky, connecting the faraway mountains to a house of the village. At that the same moment, a clear and loud crying of a baby was heard from the rainbow, breaking the silence of the morning.

With the strange phenomenon surrounding his birth and the background of his family, the ninth successor of the family, Lobsang Tenzin attracted attention of Thomjong Lama, a great living Buddha of Nyingma School. After a long and complicated religious ritual, the three-year-old boy was nominated by Thomjong Living Buddha as a reincarnated living Buddha of a monastery of Nyingma School in Nayu. He named the boy "Pema Norbu" (born of the lotus). And the monastery was named Nyizin (unsetting sun).

There was a legend about the naming of the monastery. When the monastery was about to be built, Master Padmasambhava asked the first abbot of the monastery to finish the construction in 38 days. The abbot racked his brains but couldn't figure out any way to complete the construction in such a limited period.

He said as much to Padmasambhava that unless the sun did not set, it was impossible to fulfill his request. Master Padmasambhava agreed: That's no problem. So he cast a magic spell and held the sun on the top of the mountain. As soon as the monastery was finished, the sun set.

The little living Buddha Pema Norbu started to learn Tibetan and to recite some simple scriptures at the monastery. Pema Norbu began reading Padmasambhava's work *The Virtue of Human Wisdom*, which has over 380 pages. In addition to daily study, the little living Buddha was asked to attend various religious activities and give blessings to believers on festivals. Three years later, Pema Norbu was six and had acquired the solemn facial expressions of a religious leader.

One day, the living Buddha Thomjong visited Nyizin Monastery with Pema Norbu's father. His father said that the political situations were not stable. Though Pema Norbu was a living Buddha, he was still very young, and his father was concerned for his safety. He planned to move to Lhasa and wanted his son to come with them. Pema Norbu was very happy to do so as he missed his parents.

In 1952, the People's Liberation Army (PLA) entered Tibet's capital Lhasa, in accordance with the Agreement of the Central People's Government and the Local Government of Tibet on Measures for the Peaceful Liberation of Tibet (or 17-Article Agreement) signed in 1951. It marked a new chapter in the history of Tibet. The plateau that had slept for thousands of years now awakened to new reality.

"New China", "the Communist Party of China", "the PLA soldier", "liberation", "the red Hans" and other new words passed from mouth to mouth. Rumors of all sorts spread across the mountains and waters like gusts of wind.

Few knew exactly what happened because life had not changed.

Three Roving Doctors

All these left little impression on the seven-year-old Pema Norbu, who instead became deeply impressed with his father's medical practice. Before the move to Lhasa, the two began to travel around helping cure patients.

The first patient had a big tumor on his head. At first, when the tumor was the size of an egg, the patient begun seeing doctors and asking monks to cast spells. All were useless. The tumor later grew as big as his head and to prevent the neck from breaking, the patient had to stay in bed everyday.

Pema Norbu's father asked the patient to sit on a chair, tied him to a pillar, shaved off all the hair, then used a boiled mixture of saline, elm bark and bamboo leaves as well as Tibetan distilled spirits to clean the entire head and the tumor. Then he put a surgical knife, once he sterilized it, into the fire, dipped it directly into the spirits and gave a cut directly in the middle of the tumor. In a second, a rotten smell and liquid came out of the tumor.

Pema Norbu's father concentrated on squeezing the tumor, as if he had not smelled anything at all. After squeezing out all liquid, he then took up a dove's feather to clean the wound, and added the powder of bear gall to it.

After seven days, the wound healed. After one and a half months, the scalp of the patient was back to normal. The patient was given a second life. People asked for the prescription, but Pema Norbu's father answered that it came from a dream.

The second was at Milindongduo. There they met with three men and a woman who were suffering from severe syphilis which was impossible to cure. Local government officials had put them into jail and planned to exile them to the mountains.

Pema Norbu's father volunteered to offer medical assistance. The next morning, Pema Norbu's father took his son to the jail. Their diagnosis showed that they were in the late stage of syphilis.

Pema Norbu's father asked his son and the patients' families to fetch some ants' eggs and baby scorpions. He mixed them with a kind of blue flower, smashed, wrapped in cloth and steamed them into liquid herbal medicine. He asked the patients to drink the medicine and washed the infected parts as well.

After several weeks, the patients recovered. The fame of Pema Norbu's father spread. Patients from all directions came to see him.

That autumn, a pregnant woman suffered a lot due to an abnormal childbirth. The woman, bleeding and in great pain, was carried to the doctor by her family. Pema Norbu's father mixed fennel, bibo and costus root with *tsamba*, added some stillingia oil, and wrapped this up with a white cloth. He put the medicine on the belly of the woman, then burned musk wrapped in Tibetan paper to smoke the acupoint of Yongquan on the underside of the pregnant woman's feet.

He asked the woman to bend and added the steamed medicine on her acupuncture point at her lower back. He repeated the process several times, and the woman gave birth to a baby at last. The mother and the child both were saved.

These cases left deep impressions on the seven-year-old Pema Norbu. Pema Norbu developed a strong longing for the mystical force in medicine—to bring the dying back to life. He had great admiration for his father, who was still in his prime of life. Spontaneously he began identifying medicine, assisting his father, and carefully observing his father's medical practice. The father taught him some basic pharmacology and medical knowledge. From that moment, Pema Norbu became a successor of the family's heritage of Tibetan medicine.

After several months, Pema Norbu's father received a messenger from an eminent family of Lhasa. The messenger presented a *hada* (silk blessing scarf) to Pema Norbu's father with great respect. He was the second housekeeper of the great noble family of Tsarong in Lhasa.

The Tsarong's youngest son, who studied in India, suffered from a rare splenopyretic disease. Though he had seen many Indian doctors, the disease remained uncured. They decided to consult doctors of the Tibetan-inhabited areas, but few doctors had any experience with such a disease.

Then they heard about Pema Norbu's father. They knew that he was from the respected medical family of Qiemo, and that he, his father and grandfather had visited India and studied there. Perhaps Pema Norbu's father might have an answer.

The family invited Pema Norbu's father to Lhasa and prepared the transportation for him and his family to come. Considering they were planning to go to Lhasa anyway, Pema Norbu's father discussed this with his wife and then agreed.

The family traveled about 20 days before arriving at the Potala Palace. When they arrived in Lhasa, the Tsarong family arranged for Pema Norbu's father to go to India, and for his wife and eight-year-old Pema Norbu to settle in Lhasa.

In early 1950s, Lhasa was only a fraction of its present size. It still was a flourishing capital city to Pema Norbu, who had only spent time in the countryside. Vendors, beggars and tramps, honor guards of nobles, officials riding horses in streets and alleys, dazzling shops on Barkhor Street…all these scenes attracted him. In addition, he could sometimes see some PLA soldiers. But for Pema Norbu they were just one of the many scenes in Lhasa.

Pema Norbu's father arrived in India and found that the son of the Tsarong family was dying. Pema Norbu's father didn't fail the Tsarong family and brought the son back to life with his superb medical skills. Unfortunately, he became infected with the disease, but he missed his wife and son, so he rushed back to Tibet while still ill. Years later, the incompletely cured disease finally took the life of the eighth successor of the Qiemo family.

Pema Norbu's mother stayed with the Tsarong family. They also arranged for Pema Norbu to study writing and literature at the family monastery of Tsarong.

This was not like his monastery. As head of the Nyizin Monastery, the little living Buddha was worshiped everyday. When he studied Tibetan, an acolyte would help him turn pages of the books.

It was different in Lhasa. There were many living Buddhas here and monasteries were full of eminent monks. He had to start over from the beginning. Fortunately because of this Pema Norbu was able to consolidate what he had learned and enrich his knowledge.

As the sacred and political center of Tibet, Lhasa was full of activities, which always involved the Tsarong family. Soon after Pema Norbu's father came home to Lhasa in 1952, some great living Buddhas of Nyingma School came from Xikang area, and one of them was a relative of the Qiemo family.

The Tsarong family brought out Pema Norbu and his father to welcome them. They were invited to Tsurphu Monastery and met with the greatest living Buddha, the 16th Karmapa of the Black Hat Sect of Karma Kagyu of Tibetan Buddhism.

Karma Kagyu is the ancient school of Tibetan Buddhism which created the reincarnation system of living Buddhas. As the school had absorbed much of Tibetan indigenous culture, it also had a profound knowledge of astronomy, calendric calculation and Tibetan medicine.

The 16th Karmapa and Pema Norbu's father discussed prescriptions and pathology. Though Pema Norbu didn't understand much of the conversation, he listened attentively and his desire to become a doctor intensified.

They lived seven days in Tsurphu Monastery and it left a deep impression on the little boy. When they left, the 16th Karmapa told his father that his son had a bright future and will benefit the people. He gave Pema Norbu a new name: Qiemo Chonyi Gyatso.

Not long after he returned to Lhasa, his father felt that so many social activities restricted his medical practice. Plus, he needed to take care of himself, so he wanted to go home. The Tsarong family suggested the family move to Drigung, because a son of the family was a living Buddha of Drigung Thel Kloster, and owned a manor.

Pema Norbu's father accepted this proposal, brought his wife and son to Drigung, and lived at Er Manor.

Rite of Passage

Drigung lies to the northeast of Lhasa, under the jurisdiction of Medro Gongkar. Drigung Thel Kloster is an imposing monastery with many monks. It is well known for its altar of celestial burial. It is said that the altar of celestial burial there has a golden pathway to India. People believed that the souls of the dead sent to the altar would reach nirvana. Therefore, almost everyday the mountainous path to Drigung Thel Kloster was full of groups sending their dead to be cremated.

Pema Norbu's family settled in Er Manor, about 10 kilometers away from the monastery. While his father practiced medicine he also took charge of some of the management of the manor. Pema Norbu was sent to the monastery and studied together with a son of the Tsarong family.

This period was quite peaceful. Every once in a while, Pema Norbu would ask for his mother's permission to go home to Er Manor and visit his father and sometimes his father would go to Drigung Thel Kloster to cure ill monks. At every meeting, the father asked about his son's study and taught him what medical knowledge he could understand.

Two years later in the autumn of 1955, Pema Norbu's master went back to his own monastery. He took Pema Norbu along with him. They visited ancient monasteries of different schools along the way.

When they reached Yangregang, it was the Tibetan Year of the Monkey and the "phowa" ceremony was held. The "phowa" ceremony is conducted by eminent monks to enable passage to Buddhahood through the casting of "phowa" spells for the dead. After the ceremony, the living Buddha recruited 30 talented young monks for induction.

These candidates, ranging between 8 and 13, needed to pass multiple tests. First their former three generations should not be butchers, artists, handicraftsmen or blacksmith, and have no reports of evil behaviors. Next the young monks should have good features, physical agility and a ready tongue. Then a living Buddha looked over each one. It was also necessary to examine the family so a family member was asked to come and answer questions. This needed to be certified by someone with certain social status and creditability. Led by his master, Pema Norbu went through these preliminary tests. The living Buddha Tsarong Tsering, a son of the Tsarong family, testified about his family background.

Pema Norbu was among the 35 candidates. His father was happy to hear that his son was chosen by the living Buddha. He sent a letter, telling the son not to fail the living Buddha.

The master monk told them how to complete the next two stages. The first stage was the practice of self-denial which would last 90 days. After that the monks could be guided towards their particular mission, according to their own talents and gifts. In a word, it was a chance of a lifetime.

The young monks started to prepare for the abstinence rite. They first took a shower, changed into new clothes and stopped eating anything that was alive. After several days, they cleaned their stomach by drinking rhubarb water. Some weakened ones were unable to continue and only 17 remained.

Pema Norbu was one of them. Another seven days passed. The candidates were allowed to drink three mouthfuls of water and take three pills. After three days the abstinence rite officially began.

The place for the practice of self-denial was neither mystical nor far away from human inhabitants. It was below the monastery.

There were a number of small rooms, about four square meters each. They were built of stone, with smooth walkways and floors of flattened soil. There were no desks and chairs nor windows, only a rope hung down from the ceiling. It was connected to the room of the monk supervising the rite. If someone couldn't take the trial any longer, he could pull the rope. The bell tied at the other end of the rope would be heard by the supervising monk who would immediately come and open the door. He could leave but it meant that he was eliminated.

On the morning of an auspicious day, the 17 young monks were taken to these rooms. Before the doors were sealed, the master monk provided each with a plate and a copper pot. On each plate were 90 butter balls as big as pigeon eggs. In the pot was half a container of water.

The lamas told them to eat one butter ball and one drop of water every day. More would be considered reason to be eliminated. After these words the monks sealed the doors.

In the 90 days, 12 more monks failed. They pulled the rope bell and were rescued. Three died of hunger and cold. Perhaps they thought to pull the rope, but were too exhausted to be able to do it, or passed out before they realized they needed to quit or die.

After 90 days, those who quit were encouraged by the living Buddha and sent back to their respective monasteries. For those dead, the living Buddha held a grand ceremony to release their souls from purgatory, and proclaimed that they were on their way to Buddhahood.

Two finally made it through the dark days and nights and walked out (or were taken out, rather) of the small rooms. Pema Norbu and another 13-year-old young monk. The living Buddha asked them about what they saw and what they heard in their hallucinations to determine their ranks.

Their accounts were almost the same, and the process of the feelings and hallucinations were the same as well. The only difference was that the 13-year-old little monk saw Buddha Sakyamuni and described the scene in detail. Therefore, he was placed on the first rank while Pema Norbu was second. The lama of the first rank now lives in the United States of America. His memory of this past experience is still fresh.

Lobsang Tenzin (Pema Norbu) described the feelings of the rite in detail.

"The room for abstinence rite was very small. After the door was sealed, it was completely dark. After a long time, my eyes adapted to the darkness and I saw my body from several faint streams of light through tiny holes. The fear of such an isolated world suddenly snapped my heart. To resist such feelings, I kept chanting incantations of Padmasambhava till I fell asleep."

After he woke up, he felt hunger and thirst at first. He looked at the plate of butter ball and half pot of water and remembered the words of the lama. He picked up a butter ball, put it in the mouth. He did not swallow it, but slowly let it melt.

It was like that. He chanted scriptures and meditated when he woke up. He chanted all scriptures he had learned again and again. The first dozen of days were the toughest. The agony from thirst and hunger was unbearable, making him ache all over. Sometimes he sat cross-legged, sometimes he lay down, and sometimes he rolled on the floor.

After about 20 days, he passed out from time to time. In those trances he felt that his flesh was gone, leaving only his ribs, fingers and toes. After about 30 days, his eyes were tired and he couldn't see things clearly. After about 40 days, he couldn't open his mouth and make a sound because the throat felt stuck together. After about 50 days, he felt that he was only a skeleton with two blood vessels, red and white, pumping lightly. After about 60 days, it was like the skeleton had collapsed, leaving only a mass of entrails. After about 70 days, he felt like he had vanished. None of the body existed, only the air around him.

At the very end, his soul was flying. It flew out of the room, floated in the endless sky and stopped at a park with exotic plants and flowers. He stood on a leaf, enjoying the warm sunshine, fresh grass and sweet fragrance of flowers. The dewdrop on the leaf tasted sweet and all kinds of rare fruits were sent to his mouth by breezes, easing his hunger and thirst. The night did not fall for a long time, as if it would forever be warm, bright and harmonious. He felt very comfortable, both mentally and physically, and such coziness grew and grew, filling the entire world between the heaven and the earth. Suddenly looking back, he saw a new monastery, with red walls, gold tiles and surrounded by colorful clouds. But he didn't see any lamas. The monastery stood there silently. At that moment, he felt he was falling from the sky into a black hole. He lost consciousness.

On the 90th day, he was taken out by monks and he began to recover consciousness. On the 91st day he felt the wind was strong and the whispers of monks were like thunder rumbling from distant places. He ached all over.

He was carried into a warm house. Monks covered him with blankets and started to feed him milk, one spoon at a time and a dozen times a day. Seven days later he could sit up cross-legged. He began to eat some liquid food and recover his hearing, eyesight and sense.

The 13-year-old lama and he had the same progression of experiences. When they recovered fully, the living Buddha asked about their feelings at different stages of the abstinence rite. He answered truthfully.

When the 13-year-old lama said he saw Sakyamuni, the living Buddha listened attentively and then asked: Did you hear what Buddha said to you? He answered that he didn't hear the Buddha talking but just saw the Buddha.

The living Buddha said with a mild regret, saying that if you can hear the Buddha talking to you, then you are beyond everyone in this mundane world. Only the former disciples of the Buddha can hear him preaching. It was not easy for you to meet the Buddha. It means that you have a promising future as long as you continue your good work. His family went abroad in late 1950. He now works at the US International Institute of Life Science engaged in life science research.

The two lamas were sent to Nyimajiare, a villa attached to the monastery, for further study. Pema Norbu wanted to visit home before the study, but his request was refused. The teachers said he should first study for three months. The study included more Tibetan grammar and writing, astronomy and calendric calculation, and then the development of medical skills, *qigong* and painting. Pema Norbu's specialization was medicine, and his teacher is a Bhutanese, named Bhutan Tsering.

Bhutan Tsering was about 60 years old, with superb medical skills and a good reputation in Drigung. He had also heard of the Qiemo family, and knew that Pema Norbu was its designated rein. He was very glad to have him as his disciple.

He taught Pema Norbu about medicine for almost two months. Just as he was concentrating on these subjects, he received a letter from Living Buddha Tsarong. The letter said his father was very ill and wished his son to return home immediately.

Carrying the Heritage of the Qiemo Family

Pema Norbu spent an entire day riding home along the mountainous roads. When he reached his home in Er Manor, it was already dark. Hearing the dog barking, his mother opened the door and let her son in.

Pema Norbu saw his father sitting cross-legged on the rug, reading medical books under an oil lamp. He looked fine. He looked at his son and said slowly after a while, "I never imagined that you would be here. I thought you would be in heaven now. Now that you are here, you must have been eliminated from the rite."

Pema Norbu hurried to take out the certificate granted by the living Buddha and presented it to his father with both his hands. His father read the certificate several times. His eyes shone and he stood up and held Pema Norbu in his arms, kissing him all over. He asked his wife to kowtow to the son and chanted scriptures. After he became calm, he asked his wife to make tea for their son and held Pema Norbu's hand and sat together with him on the rug. When he learned that it was the living Buddha Tsarong who sent the letter to the son to ask him to come home, he became silent for some moments.

He said: "After nine days, I will leave this world. No one can save my life. When the first star comes out in the 9th evening, I shall leave. But until then you can not leave me for a second. You are the 9th generation of our medical family which has made historical contributions in medicine over the past 500 years.

"As far as I know, all our medical journals have been saved and recorded using serial numbers. They are the medical experiences and prescriptions of our ancestors as well as your grandfather's and mine. The prescriptions are from central China, India, Sikkim, Nepal as well as those of living Buddhas of various schools in Tibet. They are far too precious for just one doctor. Unfortunately, some of the first, second and third sets of these journals have been lost…because of the chaos of wars. They were buried underground or hidden in monasteries and now no one knows where to find them.

"I have practiced medical service for more than three decades. I have mastered the contents of some of the family's medical journals and accumulated my own prescriptions. Many have been improved by me because I took into account changes in the geology and climate where the patients reside. These prescriptions number more than 300, which will be of great benefit.

"In addition, I have eight core secret prescriptions of the family's first medical journals. They are general principles for classifying different categories of diseases. They can be divided into 200 single prescriptions. But I only pass you 198. The other two rely much on chanting of scriptures and incantation. I keep them to myself, because you need to be accomplished, otherwise they will not help cure the patients and even bring harm to yourself."

Then Pema Norbu's father gave a huge silvery *kawu* (a treasure box containing scriptures, images of the Buddha, etc.) to him, saying that the most essential documents were contained in it. In these last days, the father taught him their unique pulse diagnosis methods, the identification of some rarely-seen herbs and a secret prescription for medicinal preparations. He particularly focused on three key points: ethics, self-improvement and self-practice.

On the sixth day, his father asked Pema Norbu to sit cross-legged the whole night and clear his mind.

On the night of the seventh day, the father said to him, "I have taught everything to you, but you may not remember it all. For the next three days and nights, I will help you remember everything. He told Pema Norbu to sit in front of the image of the Tibetan Saint of Medicine Yutok Yonten Kongpo and he sat back to back with him.

He repeated the secret prescriptions for various diseases and used his power to help his son remember. When Pema Norbu would get sleepy, he would prepare and feed his son herbal soup. On the ninth night, Pema Norbu was surprised to see that his father and he had changed position. He had faced to the north wall, but now he faced the south wall while his father was facing the Tibetan Saint of Medicine.

His father asked Pema Norbu's mother to sleep in another room. At midnight, he chanted incantations while he slapped Pema Norbu's back. The slapping was so hard that Pema Norbu's head almost hit the wall. Pema Norbu felt that his body was beginning to burn and his limbs go numb but then his brain expanded.

His father asked him to turn around, but he couldn't move. His father gave him a bowl of cool liquid medicine. He drank it and slowly his fever went away and his body moved.

When he turned around, he saw something before him which was covered by a piece of red cloth. His father unveiled the cloth. There were a dozen Buddhist relics the size of small pearls.

His father told him to swallow them but not to let them touch his teeth or they would lose their effects. Then he asked his son to have a butter ball. After all these, his father told him that his brain was still locked.

"The keys are the three points of ethics, self-improvement and practice as I told you before. If you fail to do that, the lock will remain locked. Only by hard work can you find the best chances to open the lock.

"You should remember that it is your ethics and practice that will save your career and even your life. Your patients will save you. My soul, the souls of the Qiemo family, and the souls of great doctors will help you.

"But if you do wrong and contaminate your soul, we won't be able to save you. For every secret prescription I pass down to you lies a soul. You can experiment with them with a bold heart."

Then his father gave him five restrictions: first, no alcohol; second, no lies; third, no request of money from patient but you may accept it if they give it to you voluntarily; fourth, no flirting with female patients; fifth, no bargaining over the price of medicine, just take whatever the patients give you.

After he finished these, he focused on the word "dear." He said, "The dearest people are your parents, but they will die. But tens of thousands of patients won't die. As a doctor, the dearest people should be your patients. Whenever and wherever your patients need you, you should go to them without hesitation, even if you are sick. When you cure the disease for your patient, it will also relieve your own pain."

His words became the principle of Pema Norbu's medical practice.

On the afternoon of the ninth day, Pema Norbu's father asked him to call his mother.

He said, "Mix saffron and musk with butter to tuck into the nine holes of my body when I am dying. Bury me in water instead of a celestial burial or cremation. Bury me on the third day. Use cloths of two colors to wrap up my body. Use white cloth for the upper part and blue cloth for the part below my waist. After three days, have a look at my head. If it has bled, carry me for water burial.

"My son shall hold my head and find some young people, born in the year of dragon and horse, to hold my body when it is carried downstairs. Use a white horse or yellow horse to carry me.

"For the three days when my body is at home, don't tell anyone. After that you can tell people." At this moment, Pema Norbu's mother was choked with sobs. Pema Norbu was crying on his father's body. But his father was calm. He said he felt relieved. It was the Buddha's delight to allow him to say these last words to his son! It's getting dark. "Go out and have a look at the stars. I am leaving."

Pema Norbu's mother went out of the door. Holding his father's hand, Pema Norbu watched his father falling into dreams as if he were sleeping. It was getting dark, and his mother came to the door several times. She dared not enter the room, but turned around and went outside again with tears.

Suddenly, Pema Norbu's father opened his eyes, looked outside of the window, and said: "There is the star."

After these words, he died.

After his father died, Pema Norbu went back to study in Nyimajiare. After one year, upon the recommendations of teachers, he returned to Lhasa again.

January 1956 was the turning point for him. The 12-year-old boy was selected to study medicine at what was then called the Commission of Ethnic and Religious Affairs. At that time, his curriculum included: cultural knowledge, Buddhist philosophy, politics, traditional Chinese medicine,

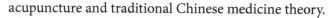

acupuncture and traditional Chinese medicine theory.

This was the first time he systematically studied traditional Chinese medicine. After three years of study, he had the preliminary foundation of TCM, and started outpatient services, which marked the beginning of his career as a doctor. In the meantime, he changed his name to Lobsang Tenzin.

In the decades of his medical practice, Lobsang Tenzin has never forgotten the last words of his father. When he applies the secret prescriptions of his family he always applies them on himself or on his family members first. He believes that he still needs to test it to make sure that it is right for his patients. In this way he obeyed his father's instructions.

Since early 1990s, Lobsang Tenzin has become famous. Patients come to his home in an endless stream. They come with hope and leave with appreciation and joy.

Lobsang Tenzin has no regular medicine academic qualifications but now he is a member of Ulcer Branch Committee of the Chinese Medical Association of the Integration of Traditional and Western Medicine, a member of External Therapy Committee of the Chinese Medical Association, and executive director of the Tibet Branch of the Chinese Medical Association.

In September 2000, the Second Balance Acupuncture Medicine Conference awarded him "Outstanding Balance Acupuncturist of the 20th Century". In April 2001, the Organizing Committee of 21st Century Natural Medicine Conference of the United Nations World Peace Foundation conferred on him the "Internationally Distinguished Doctor" award, "International Award for Natural Medicine" and "Natural Medicine Award." In April 2004, he received a doctorate degree from United Nations University for Peace at the 42nd International Natural Medicine Conference. He is the director of the Lhasa Institute of Plateau Biology.

Jiling Kezhu, Voice of the People

By Liao Dongfan

In the summer of 1981, the Tibet Federation of Literary and Art Circles organized a training course on folk literature. After the lecture section, the participants spread out to do fieldwork across Tibet.

I started my interviews from the eastern foot of Qiumo Kala Snow Mountain, along the southern bank of Brahmaputra River, and from one village to another. In mid-July, I went to Zhalang County in Lhoka. According to many, a young man named Kezhu, who lived in Jiling on the south side of the county, had a deep and thorough knowledge of Tibetan language and literature. In addition he has recorded and collected many folk stories, legends, as well as popular ballads.

Looking for Kezhu

I borrowed a horse and headed for the town of Jiling to look for this mysterious person. It was a sunny day with intermittent rain showers. The shining raindrops spread over the fields and hills like pearls. In front of me as

I rode, was a flashing and bubbling stream playing the music of a summer day on the plateau. The wet hills alongside the road gave off fresh scents. There were remains of pagodas and monasteries everywhere, indicating a cultural and religious history.

I came across a group of white buildings, which were surrounded by high walls and a wide, deep ditch. I was told it was the former Jiling Cuoba Monastery and now served as the government office.

Walking into the building, I asked a cook about the man called Kezhu. He was quite hospitable and pointed to a small single cabin. Entering the small cabin, I saw a young man in his 20s who was weaving carpet on a machine. He must be Kezhu, I thought. He has a big head with black, deep eyes. When he saw me, he hurried to greet me.

A lady in her 50s came out of the back room and gave me a bowl of wine made from highland barley. She must be Kezhu's mum. The wine was yellow-green, tasted sweet and sour, and refreshed me a lot.

I came straight to the point, "Kezhu, I heard people in the county say that you have collected quite a lot of ballads, stories and legends. Can you show me some?"

From the Tibetan cupboard he took two thick books and passed them to me.

He smiled shyly and said: "I wrote these when I had spare time in the slack season. They are recorded randomly. Excuse my poor writing!"

I read a few pages. The handwriting was quite fine. It was beautiful, neat, well-organized and easy to see as a work of art. I asked Kezhu to read several stories for me.

He read "Puppet Statue" and another about "King Sazuo," which were both popular folk stories from Lhasa and Lhoka. Then he read me a love story, which had these verses at the beginning:

Marriages of men,

Were not destined in their former lives;

Young men in Shigatse,

Young girls pasturing in northern Tibet,

Meet at the temple fair in Tashilunpo Monastery,

And marry in Nyingchi.

This is part of a long story about a young man who was in pursuit of love and happiness. It is full of twists and turns. The wording is exquisite and the emotions deep. It is written in prose for narration. It has the metrical style of *Snyan-ngag*, and the fine belle-letters of Tibetan literature for the dialogues, making the whole story like a poem.

I smiled and said after he finished reading: "Did you write this?" I asked,

Kezhu did not deny it, saying: "Sometimes I feel it is not enough to just record the words of others. I need to speak with my own voice."

Then he read a few stories and local ballads. I wanted to spend more time with him.

I suggested: "Kezhu, I will stay a couple of days in Zhalang. Could you help me with some interviews about the lives of people and how they use art and culture? Could you help me record them in Tibetan? I will do it in Chinese."

Kezhu agreed quickly. I could tell he was doing it quite willingly. First we visited a blacksmith named Baima. He had just finished making some farm tools. The job made him look like a piece of dark burnt wood. He cleaned himself in a river and returned to talk to us.

He said: "In the past blacksmiths were looked down upon. We made swords and weapons, so we were considered to be dirty murderers as well. No one would have a cup of tea or liquor with us. We were only allowed to marry daughters of our own kind. My wife's father was a blacksmith too."

Baima's wife, a robust middle-aged woman, came up and poured butter tea for us. Kezhu and I both drank like a horse which made the couple quite pleased.

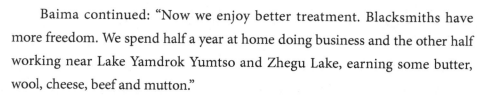

Baima continued: "Now we enjoy better treatment. Blacksmiths have more freedom. We spend half a year at home doing business and the other half working near Lake Yamdrok Yumtso and Zhegu Lake, earning some butter, wool, cheese, beef and mutton."

We left the blacksmith, went to a water mill by a small river and visited Lobsang Gyaltsen, owner of the mill. He was making *tsamba*, the traditional barley cake of Tibet, which is a staple food but also possesses deep spiritual value. So when we found him, he was white all over, in hair, beard and even his pants. He patted himself off with a cloth bag.

This is a wizened and wiry old man, with a prominent nose, tiny eyes and three teeth in his mouth. He was said to be a man of silver tongue, humor and vitality. He could tell stories, sing Tibetan opera and *zhega* (one of the oldest performing arts in Tibetan area. The word "zhega" originally referred to door-to-door folk artists singing songs expressing good wishes during the New Year and other happy occasions.). People call him "the living Argudunba."

Villagers like to come here to grind *tsamba* or just to relax. The water mill is the public space and news center of Jiling. Kezhu recorded many stories and ballads here.

Sitting beside Lobsang Gyaltsen, I felt comfortable and at ease. I have seen so many people like him in Tibet.

He said: "My father was a *duiqoin* (small households with chimneys emitting smoke who had no means of production or personal freedom, and the survival of each of them depended on tilling plots for the estate-holders) and so am I. I became a servant when I was 10. I herded sheep every day but I didn't even have a pair of shoes.

"The life was tough, so I ran away. I ran to Lhasa and then became a soldier. Unfortunately I was recognized by the platoon commander who came from my hometown. He told my master who took me home and I had to live another four bitter years with him.

"I heard that PLA were building highways in Nyingchi. They treated the poor well and paid them in cash. So I climbed Samye Guogela Mountain in secret and got to Gongbo Gyamda where the project was under way. I spent four years building highways there and another two years in Medro Gongkar.

"On the construction site, I danced *Sgor-Gzhas* (Tibetan group dance) twice a day. Gongbo has thick forests so it is easy to find firewood. We finished work early and took a bath. Then we lit a campfire and everyone started dancing. We danced from dusk to dark, from dark to dawn. The PLA soldiers enjoyed the dancing as well.

"Once people from Lajiali suggested a competition with Zhalang workers. They were seven from Lajiali but from Zhalang there was just Wujian and I. The competition lasted five or six hours. We competed to see whose dancing gestures were better and who sang longer and without repetition.

"We won. We were given a bar of soap, a box of sugar, a carton of cigarettes and a pair of leather shoes as rewards. We divided the things into equally two packs for each one of us. But both Wujian and I wanted the shoes so we drew for our luck. I turned out to be the luckier one. It's the first pair of leather shoes in my life.

"Our boss, Zhu Lin, was a good man. He let us work early and knock off early so that we could dance. In addition, I was extremely happy at the moment when we got paid. On payday, everybody sat on the grass as the PLA soldiers brought out the trunks of silver dollars. They put the trunks in the middle and the shining dollars were so flashy that they hurt our eyes.

"We cried and shouted, sang and danced. We also took off our Tibetan robes and threw them into the air. The PLA soldiers would call a name and that person got up to get his pay. Some put their money in their clothes, some in ragged hats. I got the most silver dollars, ranging from 80 to 100 each time. I

counted them and their number seemed to be countless. When I went to sleep, I clinked these dollars for fun. It was the happiest thing in the world.

"I worked year after year on the construction site. Some workers came and went, but not me. Someone said to me: 'We are like the water in the river, flowing all the time; but you are like the rock on the river bed, stable and steady.' At last the highway was finished and we had to leave.

"Zhu Lin sent us to Lhasa. We stayed together for several days with him but had to say goodbye at last. I cried, and so did he. I swear that is the first time I cried. I had over 200 silver dollars in my pocket. Zhu told me: 'Don't spend money like water. Save the money and show them to your parents. Get yourself a wife!' But I didn't listen to him. I lived in Lhasa for half a month and spent almost all the money."

The vivid narration by Lobsang Gyaltsen touched me. In early 1950s, the PLA soldiers built the Xikang-Tibet Highway (today's Sichuan-Tibet Highway) and Qinghai-Tibet Highway. Tens of thousands of Tibetans joined in the project, which left them unforgettable memories.

Li Gangfu, a writer, collected and sorted out ballads from workers on the Xikang-Tibet Highway project, and published a book titled *The Voices of People of Xikang and Tibet*. Though he was not very good at Tibetan and the translation needed improvement, the book is a mirror of the passion, life and spiritual world of workers like Lobsang Gyaltsen.

On second day, Kezhu and I visited Danpeila, secretary of the Party Branch of Xekong Commune. Danpeila was a robust man with dark skin. He was straightforward and forthright. He reveled in local folk singing and dancing.

He said: "When it comes to dancing *Sgor-Gzhas*, people of Xekong are the best in Lhoka, even in the whole of Tibet.

"Before the liberation, there was a huge temple fair in Jampaling, the biggest one in Tibet. Tens of thousands of people visit Jampaling for business, singing, dancing and fun. Every night, it was a ritual to hold *Sgor-Gzhas* dancing competitions. Every village sent their teams and the competitions were fierce. We, Xekong people, always beat all other competitors. One year, the Sakya King visited there and saw us dancing. He greatly admired and praised us with his thumbs up: 'Gandi (meaning good)! Gandi!'"

He added: "During the Cultural Revolution, an official came to Xekong and banned us from singing folk songs and dancing *Sgor-Gzhas*. He said that such practices 'should be eliminated from the root.'

"I hit the ceiling when I heard this. I said, 'Singing and dancing are roots inherited from our ancestors. They are more precious than pearls and gold. They cannot be banned. I told my mum, if there were no songs in Xekong, then Danpeila must have died; if there were no *Sgor-Gzhas* dances in Xekong, then Danpeila's two legs must have been broken!'" Danpeila said in an impassioned and forceful way.

Our hearts leaped for joy and we admired such strong love, support, determination and courage for local culture, folk singing and dancing. Then we asked Danpeila to sing some *Sgor-Gzhas* songs. Kezhu recorded the lyrics in Tibetan language and I recorded in Chinese. We were good partners. Kezhu also accompanied me to cross the Brahmaputra River to pay a visit to Samye Monastery, which was under renovation.

During my stay at Samye Monastery, Kezhu read me some lyrics of *Sgor-Gzhas* so I could translate them. These lyrics pay tribute to their hometowns, to the nature, labor, love and beautiful life. Some of them are historical stories and folklore.

Son of the Living Buddha of the Jiling Monastery

We stayed together for some days and I got to know Kezhu's family background. His father, Gongjue Qimi Jiasuo, was not an ordinary farmer, but a Grand Living Buddha of Jilingcuoba Monastery. His monastery, built by Kashmirian scholar and religious master Kaqibanqing Xiajialixi in the 13th century, was quite famous in Tibet and enjoyed a high reputation.

The Living Buddha Gongjue Qimi Jiasuo was a master of both Esoteric and Exoteric Buddhism, and proficient in Tibetan traditional culture. He was a respectable living Buddha. When he was 40, though, he fell in love with a nun from a small monastery. He was crazy about her, as if he were possessed by devil. No matter how his relatives and friends tried to persuade him to forget the love, he didn't budge a bit.

Finally he gave up his status and superior life to go away with his beloved. They lived a reclusive life in a small monastery called Gazipu. They had two sons, the elder was Bantai and the younger Kezhu. The living Buddha was not a bit regretful about what he had done. He said many times with pride: "The two sons are both the avatar of my flesh and soul; the elder brother is quiet, so he is the avatar of my static nature; the younger brother is bold, so he is the avatar of my dynamic nature." He started to teach them spelling and calligraphy. Unfortunately, when Kezhu was six, his father got ill and died, leaving the widow and the orphans, and a room of books.

At that time, the democratic reform was underway and these were tense times in Tibet. Their mother wouldn't allow them to go outside. Besides, there was nowhere for them to play in such an isolated place. Kezhu and Bantai, beside reading and writing, explored their father's books.

Some days later a lama walked into their home and married their widowed mother. He was also an educated man. Under the guidance of the stepfather, Kezhu began reading *The Life Story of Padmasambhava* and other Tibetan classics at the age of eight. He started to write using many styles, including *Snyan-ngag*.

The two brothers grew up. During the Cultural Revolution, a group of activists intruded into the Gazipu wood and found the forgotten corner, as well as the wife of a living Buddha and their children. The mother and children were moved to Jiling. The brothers were put to work; the elder on a reservoir construction site and Kezhu on a collective farm. Kezhu was happy actually to quit such a solitary life and to live and work with other young men and women.

He was brilliant and a quick learner on the farm, particularly with his hands, enabling him to build a house with his elder brother. Kezhu became interested in stories and folk ballads told and sung by villagers. He recorded them in his spare time. He even wrote new lyrics and shows for the local art troupe to perform.

In this way Kezhu became famous. Local people would ask for his opinion on many things, such as the naming of a child, or a date for marriage or funeral. Some even honored him with Living Buddha Kezhu, and asked him to give them blessings.

Selling *Pulu* in Street of Lhasa

At Samye Monastery, I called Zhang Yuemin, head of Tibet Federation of Literary and Art Circles, and told him about Kezhu. I asked him to allow me to bring Kezhu to Lhasa.

Zhang agreed since he said that it was our responsibility to discover and make full use of talents, especially talents in the Tibetan language. Zhang thought Kezhu might be able to help consolidate Tibetan folk art.

Kezhu and I went to Lhasa. All participants in the fieldwork exercise were back too. We gathered together, sharing our experiences and feelings. We also shared the legends, ballads and songs we had collected. Kezhu told everyone about his own collection and this deepened the respect of my colleagues. Zhang attended the meeting every day and had discussions with us.

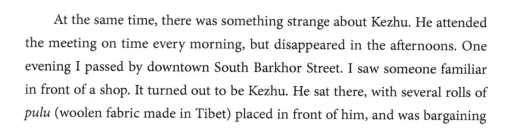

At the same time, there was something strange about Kezhu. He attended the meeting on time every morning, but disappeared in the afternoons. One evening I passed by downtown South Barkhor Street. I saw someone familiar in front of a shop. It turned out to be Kezhu. He sat there, with several rolls of *pulu* (woolen fabric made in Tibet) placed in front of him, and was bargaining with a buyer!

I went up quietly and patted him on the shoulder: "Kezhu, how's your business?" He looked up and was a bit embarrassed: "Sir, I am so sorry. My neighbors and friends asked me to sell *pulu* for them in Lhasa. I will sell all of them very soon." I did not blame on him, just told him to come back early.

After the training sessions were over, the preparatory team of Tibet Federation of Literary and Art Circles decided to recruit him to help with the collection of folk literature and arts. He looked overjoyed and smiled like an angel. He said: "I want to ask for several days off. I will go home for a couple of days to deal with some family matters."

A Noted Tibetan Writer

We did not hear from him again. I wondered how it was possible for Kezhu to fool us the way he did. Later I received a call from the Lhoka Administration of Culture, learning that Kezhu was employed as a writer for a local singing and dancing troupe. I then remembered what he had said to me when we first met. "Sometimes I feel it is not enough to just record others' words. I need to speak with my own voice." It was I who had not really "heard" him.

In 1997, two years before my retirement, I visited Lhoka again. I was warmly received by Kezhu and his colleagues from the troupe. Kezhu had become a renowned writer, whose stories and proses won lots of prizes.

Tibetan crosstalks, *zhega*, talking and singing, singing and dancing, and comedy shows he compiled were known and very popular.

That year, Kezhu won several awards including the Qomolangma Literary Award. I am so happy to see what Kezhu has achieved. He is speaking his voice from his heart and the people of Tibet are listening attentatively to it.

The First Tibetan PhD in Anthropology

Narrator: Gelek
Recorder: Jin Zhiguo

Family

My name is Gelek, a scholar and research fellow with the China Tibetology Research Center (CTRC). I am one of the first Tibetan postgraduates, the first PhD in anthropology as well the first Tibetan doctorate brought up by New China. The focus of my major – Tibetology – is the history beginning from 1950 and specializes in the different classes in Tibetan-inhabited areas. What was the society like for Tibetans? Through surveys and investigations, we think that traditional Tibet society can be regarded as a feudal serfdom society. This resembled the kind of feudalism of the Middle Ages of Europe or the Spring and Autumn and Warring States periods in China. We studied the Tibetan literature and language to find that Tibet's feudal society had changed little during the past 1,000 years.

I am glad to see that China spares no effort in maintaining Tibetan culture. Publications by the Tibetan Academy of Social Sciences are in both Tibetan and Chinese. The Chinese Academy of Social Sciences also publishes

magazines in Tibetan, Chinese and English. There are as many as 30 magazines of different kinds, many of which have a large readership.

The recent work on the ancient Tibetan books is another example.

In 1988 when I was assigned to CTRC, we began to work on the *Tripitaka*. This is a 1,000-year-old Tibetan classic that contains 97 percent of Tibetan Buddhist scriptures originally translated from ancient Indian languages. Previous editions were published by Tibetan local governments or tribal chiefs for religious purposes. We wanted to have an edition that was more scholarly so that it could continue to be a resource for the study of Tibet. The new edition has outlines in both Chinese and Tibetan as well.

Since it is a monumental project, we set up a collation department and checked the original works in Tibetan page by page. This unprecedented collation was published in 2010.

There is also an office in charge of the preservation of ancient literatare masterpiece *The Epic of King Gesar*, with branches in local areas. *King Gesar* is a Tibetan heroic epic, which has been passed down orally through the ages. It is a collection of ancient tales, legends, sayings, and various folk arts. Thus far, 150 volumes containing 1.5 million lines have been collected. Listed by UNESCO as a masterpiece of Oral and Intangible Heritage of Humanity, its 1,000-year anniversary was celebrated in 2002 and 2003. This is an example of the protection of traditional Tibetan culture and the promotion of cultural exchange. Moreover, the Government of Tibet Autonomous Region has paid great attention to seeking *Gesar* balladeers. During the past few years, it has

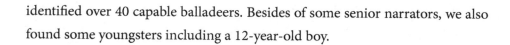

identified over 40 capable balladeers. Besides of some senior narrators, we also found some youngsters including a 12-year-old boy.

My Story

I was born in Ganzibiz Tibetan Autonomous County which is in Sichuan Province. Being a remote place on the Qinghai-Tibet Plateau, it is about 800 kilometers to the west of Chengdu and beside the Brahmaputra and the Jinsha rivers. Thanks to the improvement of communications, it is now well connected with the outside world.

I was born in 1951, the same year that the People's Liberation Army (PLA) entered Tibet. The PLA soldiers passed through my hometown Ganzibiz to Tibet. So I grew up in New China and I have witnessed the great changes since that time.

The changes date back to the democratic reform in 1959. As indicated above, Tibet had not changed much for many centuries. This reform in 1959 was similar to those in the rest of China, and it changed the relationship between peasants and the landowners. In my hometown, since we were part of Sichuan Province the reform took place in 1956.

Tibet can be characterized as a hierarchy consisting of a dozen classes. The highest class in Tibet were nobles and at the top of this nobility was the Dalai Lama. Each landowner had his own serfs, grasslands and territories. There were of course nobles in my hometown as well.

Under the nobles were three classes. These serfs made up 95 percent of Tibet's population: *tralpa* in Tibetan (namely people who tilled plots of land assigned to them and had to provide corvee labor for the serf-owners), *duiqoin* who had no land or personal freedom and the survival of each of them depended on the wealth of the nobleman, and *nangzan* who comprised five percent of the population and were hereditary household slaves. This was the lowest class and they had no lands, no houses, and their total responsibility was to be of service to the nobles all their lives. It was to this last class that my family belonged.

We lived in the hallway between the kitchen and the living room of the home of our nobleman. We had nothing but clothing and mats. My two sisters and my mother worked for the nobleman. There was no such thing as a home for us.

In my society there was no other way to live. There was not a single primary school so no way to provide better for families of serfs. The only way out was to become a soldier for the nobleman or become a monk in a monastery. A monk's major task was to study the Buddhist scriptures for 20-30 years.

Being a soldier was a possible but dangerous choice, battling to safeguard the interests of the nobles. Frequent battles occurred between different landowners because there was endless animosity between the tribes.

Having no security in our lives, we didn't realize how unequal the society was. We were taught that people were reincarnated and one's misfortune in this life was a result of evil acts in his previous life. We did not realize that there were other ways to change our circumstances.

I never saw my father. It was on my shoulders that the great expectations of my family lay. The biggest dream of my mother was that I could be someone extraordinary or go to study at a monastery. She begged the nobleman we worked for to allow her or two sisters to replace me and to let me study. According to our tradition, if a family has several children, the family is allowed to send one to the monastery as a monk. The child needs to be at least seven to ten years old.

At the age of five, I was allowed to beat the drums for prayers in the scripture hall of the noble. Though I was a servant, I was allowed to learn Tibetan. It was the start of my study.

My formative education was learning how to write. There was no paper, pen nor books. Our teacher was a monk who held a makeshift blackboard of a length of 30 centimeters. Such a blackboard was made by covering a board with old butter and stove ashes . When you finished writing you showed your work to the teacher, who would correct your mistakes. In this way, I recited the classics and learned how to write.

Liberation

The People's Republic of China was established in 1949 but not all of the provinces had become fully part of the new system at that time. It was 1950 that I first saw the PLA soldiers. It was when I was learning how to write at the monastery. A large group of men appeared in the streets outside. I had no idea who or what they were.

They came to live downstairs in the nobleman's home. I liked them because they sang and rode horses. I offered to help them in small ways and they gave me corn and rice in return. This was the first time in my life I had something decent to eat.

My hometown Ganzibiz was liberated in 1950 but for the first six years it was still ruled by nobles, with many of the traditional social institutions. Then in 1956, a group of officials arrived, encouraging children to go to school. At first many of us were reluctant to go to this school.

My mother and I knew nothing about the Communist Party of China (CPC) but my mother's greatest wish was for me to go to school. It didn't bother her which school it was.

She was the first one to register her child. Then more people followed suit. About 100 people in our village were encouraged to go to primary school.

The classroom was in a palace that used to belong to a nobleman in Ganzibiz County. My mother was illiterate so when the teacher asked about my birthday, she didn't know. The school had desks, chairs and stationary. It offered board and lodging as well.

In the first two years, a lama from the neighborhood taught us Tibetan. Literature, history and math were all taught in Tibetan. There was only one teacher for all of 100 or so students.

In less than two years Tibetan and Han Chinese teachers, graduating from colleges in central China, came and set up more classes.

The biggest problem for me was to learn the Chinese language. I was more interested in Tibetan, so my grades there were better.

From my childhood my mother taught me to study hard. When I finished Grade Five in primary school, some of us were sent to primary schools in the county seat, which is 33 kilometers from our small village, to continue their education in Chinese.

I was sent to Second Primary School. This was the first time for me to leave the village and my family. When I first walked into the county seat of Ganzibiz County and saw electric lights, real blackboards and movies, I realized the limitation of my village. It opened a new door before me to see the rest of the world.

Many students in that school spoke Chinese well. When we got there, we could not catch up at first. So the school divided the blackboard into two, with one half for the newcomers and the other half for other students. While I was learning to write the Chinese character for "man," other children were learning to make whole sentences. I envied them, so I put all my energy into study. Even in 1960, when the country was stricken by famine, I used my government food allowance for books so I could learn faster.

I took full advantage of my new life. I was one of the only two successful candidates of secondary school in our prefecture and the only one from my village.

The biggest challenges were tuition and clothes in the secondary school. I used to wear Tibetan robes all the time. I didn't know how to put on trousers.

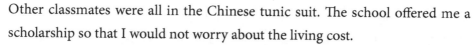

Other classmates were all in the Chinese tunic suit. The school offered me a scholarship so that I would not worry about the living cost.

Since I still spoke limited Chinese, I worked hard. For example, I volunteered to clean the classroom and help other students with their homework. For this, I was honored as an excellent student every semester.

Though my mother could not read, she was thrilled to see the seal of the school on the certificate of reward. Every vacation when I returned home, I brought home a certificate. She was proud of me, and so was I.

In early 1960s we had more famines and almost half of the students quit school within two years. I had the same dilemma: to go home or to go to school. I decided to suspend schooling given such circumstances.

Before I could carry out my decision, my mother reached school. She took me to the headmaster and told him that I was not going back. The headmaster, a kind Tibetan, said that he hadn't know I had stopped attending classes. He asked my mother to go back home and he would take care of me.

In this way I was able to continue my schooling. My Chinese got better and better. I could read books like the *Romance of the Three Kingdoms*. Upon graduating from this secondary school I was sent to school in Chengdu to attend the Southwest University for Nationalities, majoring in Tibetan translation.

Changes

During my school years in 1956-1960, many changes were taken place, including a rebellion that occurred throughout the Tibetan-inhabited areas and in particular Tibet. The rebellion flared just as the Dalai Lama came into power. Some monks instigated it. There were no men above 18 years old left in the village because of this. There were fights and battles in the neighboring hills of my hometown. The whole society was in turmoil.

For my family, however, the changes were fortunate. My mother knew she owed special thanks to the CPC because they helped her find schooling for me. She asked my sister to help the Party. We used to be at the bottom of all of the families in the village. Represented by my sister we became the backbone of the new government.

We were given a house to live in. It was a large house newly renovated for a noble. The deepest impression of mine was that there were glass windows and I could see the reflection of the electric light bulbs. In the stock house there were plenty of small pieces of butter and beef. Later we were given yaks, horses and land by the government so that we were able to cultivate our own land. For the first time the family lived by ourselves.

One night after we had dinner, we saw torches outside. We saw some PLA soldiers. They asked us whether they could live in the house for some time. Mother agreed to give them rooms upstairs. They refused, insisting to live in the stable downstairs, but my mother disagreed, Finally they agreed to live in the kitchen.

The next morning, my sister went to the kitchen to get some water. To her surprise, she found that the jar was already full. The soldiers also helped us with house chores and gave me cookies and photos as gifts. I hung around these PLA soldiers for a couple of months, before returning to school. They told me a lot about the

Gelek with his teacher Li Youyi in Lhasa, 1981

world outside. These impressions became the stimulation for me to go on to secondary school!

In 1964, I was enrolled at Southwest University for Nationalities, where I spent the first part of my university education from 1964 to 1968. Then the Cultural Revolution (1966-1976) took place and I was assigned to work in my hometown. When it was over in 1977 I returned to my university. One year later I was accepted for postgraduate studies at the Chinese Academy of Social Sciences to do academic research on the society and history of Tibet.

The policy of freedom of religious belief was reinstated in 1977 after the Cultural Revolution was over, as well as the authorization to teach and use the Tibetan language. To further protect Tibetan language and culture, the government passed a law to use Tibetan in government offices and official papers. Many Tibetan students also receive preferential treatment in education to attend universities and postgraduate courses. For example, students from Tibetan Secondary School need fewer points to get into Peking University.

Upon graduating, I first worked at the Ethnic Affairs Commission of National People's Congress. I investigated and researched about the laws of ethnic autonomous regions. Then I worked in the Great Hall of the People for three years. I continued my studies and obtained my PhD in anthropology from Zhongshan University in 1986. I then worked in Sichuan and Guangzhou provinces until I was asked to help prepare for the establishment of the China Tibetology Research Center in Beijing.

Protecting Tibetan Culture

From the time of the inception of the Red Army, the Communist Party of China has endeavored to show great respect to the poor and for local ethnic customs. In 1936, when General Zhu De and the Red Army passed our hometown, his soldiers wouldn't enter people's homes and monasteries.

There were strict rules. They put up banners which read "Freedom of Religious Belief" and posted them everywhere to ease the minds of the local people. In fact, the living Buddha in our village became a good friend of General Zhu.

Zhao Erfeng of the Qing Dynasty failed to take my hometown and so did the soldiers of Kuomintang. It was unbelievable that the Red Army made it safely across the grasslands to where I lived. They did it by talking to local people and showing them respect towards their customs. So they went through without shedding any blood.

The Red Army had several policies towards ethnic peoples. First, they respected folk customs and traditions. Second, they offered help to them. Third, they fully respected their freedom of religious belief. These were of great influence.

These three policies became the first article of the laws of the ethnic autonomous regions once the PRC was established. Through efforts by Panchen Lama and Ngapoi Ngawang Jigme, as well as the Standing Committee of the People's Congress of Tibet laws were passed to make Tibetan one of the official languages in Tibet. Meetings of all sizes should provide translation into Tibetan. TV programs should be in Tibetan as well as newspapers and signs. The *Ganzibiz Daily* in my hometown is a good example.

Freedom of Religious Belief

Tibetan-inhabited areas have been through several stages under the CPC. The first stage was during the 1930s. The Tibetan Cultural Museum collected many articles, including banners written by the Red Army on "Freedom of Belief in Tantric Buddhism." The second was the right to religious belief and the preservation of monasteries in Tibet.

After the democratic reform in 1959, there were some relatively big changes. The monasteries belonged to nobles. They were not just a place for performing religious rituals but also the property of the high-ranking nobles. Monasteries owned the largest amount of lands and serfs. In Ganzibiz, the monasteries possessed 70 percent of the assets of the entire place for example. For these reasons they were confiscated and the land and property redistributed.

With the help of the central government the Beijing Lamasery set up a Senior College of Tibetan Buddhism. Colleges of Buddhism then were erected in provinces and regions.

There has been a swelling of religious faith in Tibetan regions in recent years and pilgrimage is back. My mother used to carry me on her pilgrimages but now fewer people go by foot and more by air and rail.

The old Tibet was for so many years under a political system that combined the power of religion and state, which was against the original

Conducting research at a monastery in Aba Prefecture, Sichuan Province

intention of religion. Buddhism should help people become pure hearted, not provide power and fortune. Buddhism should serve the people.

In 1981 when I was a post graduate, the elder brother of the current Dalai Lama was invited, with his family, to visit Tibetan-inhabited areas. Vice-chairman Ulanfu met him and I was the translator. The brother told me that he had seen great changes. The whole treasury of the old Tibet somehow could not afford to build a road with a length of a dozen of kilometers. Now such roads were numerous and much longer. It was a proof that both Tibetan and Han Chinese can work well and could rely on each other.

The Dalai Lama once publicized a letter, saying "Tibetan people are living in panic." However, I see just the opposite. According to our survey, Tibetan people are pleased with the policies of freedom of religious belief, regional autonomy and with the reform and opening up of the 1980s. What they fear most is turmoil and violence that might harm a peaceful, stable and harmonious society.

The Life of Amdo Qiangba, Master of Tibetan Painting

By Lengben Cairang Emao

Amdo Qiangba, master of Tibetan painting and the first artist to create modern Tibetan art, has led an extraordinary life. Born in 1915 into a poor family, he became a lama and palmer with an extraordinary talent in painting. Later he focused his effort on portraits. He has depicted the twists and turns of Tibetan modern society. Yet this century-old man, who now lives in the Potala Palace, first went to Lhasa in the 1930s on foot.

A dynamic life in many ways can be said to represent the sublime. Yet his life was full of the *joie de vivre* that comes from thoroughly enjoying what life had to offer as well. When he took off his robes in Lhasa and walked into Barkhor Street to become a street painter, he is just an example of his extraordinary life capacity. His Thangka, or Tibetan paintings, are regarded as treasures. The huge frescoes he painted on the walls in the Potala Palace and the Norbulingka Palace are still as fresh as before. The portraits he did for so many notables are clearly coveted. Yet he enjoyed life and shared it with friends.

Amdo Qiangba, a great Thangka painter

Shepherd's First Painting Brush

Qiangba was born into an agricultural/pastoral family in Jianzha County, Qinghai Province. He had slightly curly hair and often wore a dirty Tibetan robe. He liked to sing while he took his flocks of sheep out to graze. Unlike other shepherds, he used his herding stick to draw in the dirt.

He recalled, "At that time, I had no idea what painting was. I didn't know what I was drawing. Painting meant nothing but doodling on the ground using my fingers or scribbling on rocks and walls using my stick. My family could not afford paper and pen, so I used the ground as paper and twigs as my painting brush."

At the age of seven, he took off his Tibetan robe and became a little *zhaba* (monk) in Ailong Monastery in his hometown. He began to learn Buddhist

script. He got up early, made three kowtows and then recited prayers aloud. In the morning he would learn Tibetan language. After lunch, he had time to paint. The old Lama would lovingly look at him when he drew a picture.

From time to time, he was given some paper, which was precious at that time, and ink. He drew mountains, grasslands, cattle and sheep, tilted tents and rough earthen buildings, all of which he was familiar with.

There were some faded frescoes in the monastery. Looking at them, he guessed the story in them and used his fingertips to imitate the drawing on his palm. He was the youngest and the naughtiest monk in Ailong Lamasery, yet he was diligent and smart. Though a headache in his mentors' minds, he became more and more outstanding.

Wandering to Tar Lamasery

Monastery is by nature a comprehensive academy, teaching such knowledge as philosophy, etiquette, architecture, medical science, astronomy, calendar and arithmetic, painting and sculpture.

Qiangba said: "I was not much interested in Buddhist scripts. Compared with painting, sculpture, woodwork and stonework, I feel scriptures are quite boring. I cannot focus myself on them for quite long. I feel that I need to do something more meaningful, something happier and freer."

On the surface he, like all monks, received a strict and complete traditional monastic education for more than 20 years. He wore a kind of smile that only a Lama may have. He also wrote prescriptions for local folks which he learned at the monastery.

Inside his heart, his dreams became to grow.

He said: "When I pick up the brush, I have an impulse and strange ideas occur in my mind. I don't care what I draw. I just do it quickly. Sometimes even I can't understand what I draw, let alone explain it to others. At that time

I drew mostly landscapes, but those familiar landscapes turn out to be quite strange in my drawings!"

Travel is a privilege for monks. For a young monk who has lived in a well-disciplined monastery, the most desired wish is to take his wooden bowl and walk out into the world of sunshine and smile with his companions.

Qiangba first visited Tar Lamasery. He stood for a long time under the tall and thick banyan trees. A leaf fell on his shoulder and he smiled in happiness. He saw huge frescoes. Those frescoes stretched along a corridor and he understood all of them. He met a senior painter who was mixing powders of paint. The special fragrance made him exhilarated. He hoped extravagantly that one day there might be such a big wall for him to paint and he could pour his piety, love and passion onto it.

This first travel experience, though short, opened his eyes. He saw there were thousands of Lamas in the majestic Tar Lamasery who went to even further places. Some visited the Holy Land Lhasa, some went to Buddhist mountains and temples in central China. Some even made it to India and many countries to the south of China. By the time he returned to Ailong Lamasery, Qiangba was inspired!

Self-taught Painter

In 1938, the 23-year-old Qiangba became a young aspirant in Lhabrang Monastery. As one of the six monasteries of Shamanism, Lhabrang Monastery has many precious Buddhist paintings. Almost every Buddhist painting in each hall is a monumental work, with superb techniques and rich content. For the budding Amdo Qiangba, it was a vast sea of arts.

There he enrolled into Wensi College (College of Exoteric Buddhism) at the monastery to study the Five Major Classics of the Tibetan Buddhism, which consist of 13 levels. Generally it takes at least 15 years to complete the

course. But he chose a road that no one had gone down before.

It wasn't a simple issue to paint at the monastery. Tibetan Esoteric Buddhism pays much attention to "material presence." Before painting a Buddhist image, the painter should make a wish from the bottom of his heart. Then he must enter the altar to receive an incantation to free himself from worry and care during this meditation.

Moreover, the painting should be done in a place which is clean and tidy. The painter should take a bath and put on clean clothes and not be allowed to talk to others. After it is done, the painting is only considered complete if an accomplished monk adds a finishing touch to it.

Qiangba didn't see that he could be or should be trained in such a manner. He just liked to scribble on the ground, walls and stones but when he did, his drawings always came alive like real things.

Out of Kasaya, into Barkhor Street

He decided to go to Lhasa. At that time, the only way to go there was on foot taking *tsamba* as food or dried meat if you could get it. If one is fortunate, he may encounter a caravan or a group of monks.

It is about 3,000 kilometers from Lhabrang to Lhasa and it takes months to finish the journey. The hardships are beyond imagination! The 27-year-old Amdo Qiangba, wearing a ragged kasaya, and taking along with him a small bundle of art supplies wrapped in a piece of cloth, made it to Lhasa at last.

Lhasa has vast *linkas* (garden) and swamplands but no roads. People in the city mainly lived in such areas as Barkhor Street, Lubu and Balangxue. There were many pilgrims from outer Tibet. They brought fresh life to the ancient sacred land and filled the city with contentment and joy.

The young monk was touched by the atmosphere of freedom. He spent a year in Drepung Monastery, which was on a hill to the west of the city, but in the end he decided that the monastical life was not for him. So he took off his robe, resumed being an ordinary man, and joined the many others creating lives for themselves on Barkhor Street.

Qiangba said: "Earning a life for a newcomer in Lhasa was not easy. I had to earn my own bread. There were various ways that the others did this. But for me, I had no choice but to take up my painting brush."

At the four corners to the Jokhang Lamasery were poles on which hung sacred prayer banners of all colors. People who are in charge of these poles are called "rejieba." They were his first friends in Lhasa, because he sat drawing pictures for passers-by right at one of these corners. They were quite happy to help and give him support.

No. 1 Street Painter in Tibet

People might not have known the name of this street painter in Barkhor Street, but they became very fond of his drawings.

"They thought my Thangka were vivid and the portraits lifelike. I hadn't spent much time on portraits before. I got a photo of the Dalai Lama and drew a portrait of him based on the photo. One man liked it very much and bought it. My name suddenly spread in Lhasa and even Lhalu Tsewang Dorje, local highest governor of Lhasa, heard my name and sent people to look for me everywhere."

The message from the Potala Palace indeed surprised Qiangba, who was just a nobody artist and palmer. He couldn't understand how it could have come about and was worried.

He felt relaxed after he learned that the officials wanted him to do a portrait. Using a photo of the governor, he finished the portrait in a few days. Lhalu was very satisfied with the painting, as he had never seen such a new painting style.

"Since then more people came to me, especially portraits. I earned more money. I could sell 100 *liang* of Tibetan silver for a portrait, which equaled to 5 silver dollars. That income could be exchanged for more than 30 kilograms of butter. I worked a few days a month on painting, and with the money I earned, paid for all the expenses for my friends and me! We traveled around for rest of the month. It was really a pleasurable and comfortable way to live!"

He bought suits from India with wide stripes. He grew his hair. His eyes were short-sighted so he wore a pair of dark brown glasses, which were hard to get at that time.

People paid more and more respect to him, because he had a patron living in the Potala Palace. He was not the kind of artist who created his art from adhering strictly to esoteric practices by turning down the desires of life. He was by nature a man longing for life, freedom and love. So he paid more attention to practical things and his inner desire. As a result, though he was devoted to art, he also left a little space for himself and his friends.

Renowned Imperial Painter

Amdo Qiangba became a distinguished guest of local government officials, nobles and manor owners. These aristocrats asked him to draw pictures of flowers, birds, fowls, beasts and landscapes on their Tibetan cupboards, pillars, beams and walls. Of course, what he drew the most were Thangka and frescoes, as well as the sanctified image of the 14th Dalai Lama. The former palmer turned into a member of the upper class of the Tibetan society.

After the 14th Dalai Lama took over government, Amdo Qiangba made rapid advances and became the "imperial" painter. Under instructions of the Dalai Lama, he spent a long time in Norbulingka Park, painting at the summer palace. The young 14th Dalai Lama often stood behind him, watching him

paint quietly. His frescoes, so far, have remained vivid in the tranquil and beautiful Norbulingka Park.

First Painter to Paint Mao Zedong in Thangka

In 1954 when the first National People's Congress was to convene, people were busy making souvenirs. Ngapoi Ngawang Jigme asked Amdo Qiangba to draw a Thangka of Chairman Mao as the gift from Tibetan people. This is the only Thangka portrait Chairman Mao ever received. Later he visited Beijing along with the Dalai Lama and Panchen Lama.

When the Tibetan delegation came back to Tibet, he put in a request to learn painting in Beijing. He had come across such a course, unavailable in Tibet, when he visited the Central Academy of Fine Arts in Beijing. He felt he could make further progress in arts if he used such techniques. His request was

approved, making him probably the first Tibetan to learn Western oil painting techniques. As a result, he became exceptionally good at Tibetan Buddhist paintings.

He spent one year studying in Beijing. He was at the height of his work as an artist and respected by many. He focused on religious paintings and figures. He drew many traditional home decorative paintings as well, such as frescoes like "Mongolian Taming Tiger" and "God of Wealth Holding Elephant" and a wide variety of paintings on Tibetan furniture, from cupboards to recesses for Buddha statues. He returned to Tibet in 1955, creating a new kind of art for Tibet.

Those Silent Years

In 1959, Lhasa sank into a sea of chaos. Amdo Qiangba panicked and fell ill right as the Dalai Lama fled the capital. The artist was not well prepared for such changes. He always had a peaceful disposition no matter if he was in a magnificent palace or in fire-smoked ordinary households. He decided to paint.

Then came the Cultural Revolution, during which it was a miracle that he escaped torture. He was in Lhasa at the time. He hid in a small room of the empty Drepung Monastery, and secretly drew a number of Thangka.

"It was mainly as a spiritual ballast. The paintings, done in dim lights and with fear of being caught, turned out to be more vivid. I believe it was blessed by the Buddha. If I were caught painting at that time, I was doomed!" he recalled.

There were no monks in Drepung Monastery. His former friends had left. Wearing a Chinese tunic suit with four pockets, Qiangba was sad and lonely.

Unfortunately, none of his portraits of Chairman Mao were ever found again. Those on the walls were washed away by the early 1980s. Only the hidden Thangka have remained intact. Some were given to Drepung

Monastery, some to friends and those who possess them regard them as treasures.

As for himself, he doesn't have any of his paintings. If he wants to see his pictures, he goes to the Potala Palace, Norbulingka Park and the monasteries, or pays a visit to someone who collects his works.

Resplendence in the Later Years

After the Culture Revolution ended, and especially after the policy of reform and opening up of the 1980s was adopted, Qiangba felt energetic once again.

He returned to Drepung Monastery and some of the older Lamas recognized him. Their intimate laughters echoed in front of Coqen Hall. He was reminded of the young man he once was and the unique wonderful road his life created.

In 1981, Amdo Qiangba was elected the first president of the Tibetan Artists Association. On walls and ceilings of several luxurious hotels in Lhasa, Qiangba poured his passion into paintings of the landscape of Lhasa and fairies which are always flying in his heart. At the age of 75, he married his third wife, a tall and robust woman from his hometown. The marriage somehow reminded the old man of the past. She gave birth to two children: the elder one was a daughter, 12 years old when this article was written, and the younger was a boy called Luodan, eight years old. The boy resembles his father very much in eyes and chin. Both of them are studying in Xuexin Village Primary School, on the west of the Potala Palace.

Their old father has strong love for them. He always stands on the platform, staring at them as they carry their school bags and walk into the crowds.

Little Luodan became a good assistant to his father. In the later religious works he was the model of Sakyamuni. He sat still and gracefully before him.

In these happy moments, the father and the son completed one of the most precious works of art together. The rare and real talent of Amdo Qiangba has been quite influential upon his children's growth.

Though he is already an old man, he is healthy and vigorous and walks with big strides. He likes *tsamba* that is finely ground and stewed potato noodles with some Tibetan spices. Their home is at the foot of the Potala Palace, beside the stone stairs. It has a separated Tibetan courtyard, with flowers on the edge of its walls, including Tara flowers, chrysanthemums and hollies of all colors.

Like before, he likes to visit friends in Barkhor Street and to take his son and daughter to the Potala Palace.

Amdo Qiangba Fine Arts School

Amdo Qiangba's greatest wish is to pass his accumulated knowledge and experience to the next generation. With the help from departments in the region and his friends, he founded Tibet Amdo Qiangba Private Fine Arts School, which is located in a room of the former headquarters of the Tibetan army, on the east side of the Potala Palace.

The 40-plus students are from ordinary families. Some of them are just teenagers, while some are in their 30s. Under his personal instructions, they not only learn the traditional art of Thangka but also study the unique techniques and essence of the "school of Amdo Qiangba."

This is what inspires the old man the most. He expanded the school recently and brings students to more and farther monasteries. He hopes his students will go out of Tibet and find their places in a bigger world.

Portraits of Women Mountaineers

By Sonam Tsomo, Maria Antonio
Donna & Haidegete D. Hornbeck

Known for thousands of years as Qomolangma, "Goddess Mother of the World" in the Tibetan language, Tibetans still consider the Mt. Qomolangma sacred and cherish it very much. It's believed that a large number of mountains in Tibet are places of abode for mighty and dignified goddesses. Only a few Goddess-favored Buddhist saints in history have attempted climbing them. Mira Reba, a Buddhist saint, was one of them. Riding a beam of sunlight, which later became his magic carpet for religious practice, he ascended to the top of Mount Kailash.

Then the mountaineers came. British mountaineers with special equipment such as short-nailed climbing boots were first. They challenged themselves to do the impossible. People from all over the world overcome blizzards and hazardous climbing, altitude sickness and frostbite. Many brave women joined the challengers as well. With ice axes, ropes, rock pitons and boots, they too were in constant pursuit of the pinnacle.

In July 1959, 33 Chinese mountaineers, including eight women, scaled Mount Muztag Ata (7,546 meters). By a margin of 90 meters, they surpassed

the former world record in women's mountaineering, made by a French woman mountaineer in 1955 when she climbed up Mount Jianiesi, a 7,456-meter-tall peak in Nepal. Among the eight women mountaineers were the Tibetans Xirao, Phantog, Qimi and Chamujin.

Women in the past were considered weak, needing protection from men. It has not been easy to demonstrate their power, value and perseverance. This story of their heroic attempts and strong character in the mountain climbing history is a tribute to women around the world. The Tibetan women mountain climbers also showed the same independence, fortitude, dedication, passion and wisdom.

The First Women Mountaineers

In 1961, China Mountaineering Team was jointly constituted by Beijing Geology Bureau and the army, and included 10 women members. Xirao, Phantog, Qimi and Chamujin were the Tibetan members.

The first target for the team, men and women, was Mount Kongur Tiube. The climbing was beset with hindrances, mostly snowstorms, right from the start. Despite the fact that some of their best mountain climbers participated, they failed time and again. After many such attempts, they were successful.

The expedition's progress was covered in the media. According to the book *Mountaineering in China*: "Xinhua News Agency reported that on the night of June 17, 1961, young Chinese women mountaineers erected a national flag of China atop Mount Kongur Tobe Feng, (7,595 meters) on the Pamir Plateau. Two Tibetan members of the team, Xirao and Phantog, reached the summit at 10:30 pm on the night of June 17, breaking the record of 7,546 meters made by other Chinese women climbers in 1959."

When they descended from the summit, a tragedy took place. At an elevation of 6,000 meters, a sudden snow slide rushed down on them, burying four team members. Xirao was one of the victims. Phantog, who was a member of the second team, survived the disaster but almost lost her both legs.

The Women Who Challenged Mt. Qomolangma

At the end of 1974 an expedition team aiming at Mt. Qomolangma was set up in Tibet. There were 434 team members from eight different ethnic groups, including 36 women members. Phantog was appointed vice captain of the team. The team proved themselves to be ready to take on the challenge.

Guisang's Story

Guisang was a team member with Phantog. She was trained for high altitude expeditions. Unfortunately she had an accident and hurt her feet so she was unable to make it up to the summit. Guisang joined in many successful expeditions after that. In 1999 she received the flame for the National Ethnic Games torch from the world's tallest mountain.

Guisang was born in 1957 in a village called Nanmulin near Shigatse. When she was two she was sent to her aunt in Nagchu because there was no school in Nanmulin. The Cultural Revolution broke out when she was with her aunt. Those days were really tough but she was able to attend elementary school.

One day, some army officials visited her school, looking for healthy and strong recruits. It was her last year in elementary school and with her aunt's permission, she joined the army and went to Lhasa to be a nurse.

"In 1974, the China Mountaineering Team was recruiting new members to challenge Mt. Qomolangma. I was chosen. I left Lhasa for Beijing and joined the team there. Many were already in training, including Phantog and her husband. The training was hard and arduous to prepare for the upcoming risks and dangers. When we felt we were ready, we left for the base camp of the mountain," she recalled.

It was November, when there were no other mountaineers. The river was frozen, glittering in the darkness. The imposing Mount Changtse, on the opposite side of Mt. Qomolangma set off the clear outline of the north slope.

"The base camp was situated under the glacial moraines. Our team comprised of 400 people.

Guisang, successfully climbed Mt. Qomolangma twice

Most of them were Tibetans. Some were mountaineers and others were researchers. The first team, which I was on, consisted of 12 members, including three women, if I remember correctly," said Guisang.

Her teammates, including Phantog's husband Deng Jiashan, began working in the mountains. Since the team was a large one, there were countless things to be transported, including heavy equipment of thousands of kilograms, metal ladders, ropes, tents, oxygen cylinders and food. Each mountaineer needed to carry these life support materials during the adaptation process as well. In addition, cameraman of every team needed to put cameras and other equipment in their knapsack as well.

Guisang and her teammates arrived at the last camp before the summit.

All of them waited there for the snowstorm to stop.

"We got to the Attack Camp 8,600 meters above sea level and made preparations for the last ascent. However, a sudden storm caged us in for two days. We had little oxygen and the oxygen cylinder became extremely heavy. When we ran out of oxygen and food, we decided to return.

"The whole team at the base camp was demoralized. We had tried but failed. We had already lost a member on the ascent and many were sick. We thought we were waging a losing battle."

After this news reached Beijing, the central government provided strong support. Two helicopters fully loaded with fruits and vegetables flew to Shigatse, and the supplies arrived at the base camp 10 hours later.

"This was a huge boost to the morale of mountaineers and workers at the base camp. Many were weeping tears as they first bit into an apple or ate fresh spinach, something we had not had in a long time!" said Guisang.

After a week's rest, the team's energy restored and the spirits rose again. They decided to try again. Guisang was assigned to the first team. She was in very good condition now and determined to climb to the peak. However, she was not favored by fortune.

"When we reached Camp No. 5, which was 7,790 meters above sea level, we put up our tents. It was windless and the weather was getting warmer. So we took off our boots and began melting snow to cook our meal. Just as I grasped the pot, I lost balance and fell. My feet were burnt and I had to quit the attempt.

"Changcuo, another Tibetan girl in my team, suffered from an inflammation of the throat at the same time and had difficulty in breathing. She and I descended down the mountain. Now only Phantog had a chance."

Phantog's Story

In the book *Footsteps on the Summit*, Phantog describes this last part of the ascent to the peak, she writes:

"As we started up, I remembered the words from our headquarters by radio. 'Now you are the only female mountaineer of the team, but you are not alone because you represent 40 million Chinese women. You must make it all the way!'

"It was an honor but quite a challenge. We were just 168 meters from the summit, but this was the most difficult and dangerous part. After half an hour, we reached the second stairs."

Luoze, a veteran Tibetan climber, smiled as he recalled: "Phantog was the only female mountaineer who was still able to climb. This was a key goal of this climbing mission so we wanted to help her we could.

"When we got to the Attack Camp, the last before the summit, we took a few breaths of oxygen. We took no oxygen during the last part of the climb. Instead we gave her some oxygen to help her breathe better.

"At 2:30 pm we found ourselves on a platform of

Phantog after successfully climbing Mt. Qomolangma in 1975

some 12 square meters. This is the highest point of the earth!

"Dapingcuo took out the triangulation gauge. Sonam Luobu, Ngawang Sandrol, Tsering Dorje and I fixed the flag pole and erected a three-meter high metal rack. They did scientific tests on the top."

Luoze continued: "Phantog lay down on the rack while they did physiological tests on her. I knew at the base camp that researchers were reading data. We also collected snow and rock samples for scientists."

The success was broadcast. "At 14:30 on May 27, 1975 (Beijing Time), Phantog, vice head of the China Mountaineering Team, together with eight male counterparts, reached the summit of Mt. Qomolangma, becoming the first woman in the world to reach the summit from the north slope."

On May 16, 1975, a few days before Phantog reached the summit, a Japanese women mountaineer successfully scaled the mountain from the south slope. She was Junko Tabei, vice head of Women's Mount Everest Mountaineering Team of Japan. Her merit earned her the title of the "First Woman to Conquer the World's Highest Mountain."

Phantog said: "I'm not the first woman to successfully climb Mt. Qomolangma, but I'm the first female who climbed up from the north slope, which was more dangerous. I was happy. Mountaineering means hardship and danger. The greater the hardship is, the greater the danger will be."

After her success, Phantog was elected a deputy to the National People's Congress and vice-chairwoman of the All-China Sports Federation.

In November 2000, Phantog was invited to the celebration for the 40th anniversary of the founding of the China Tibet Mountaineering Team in Lhasa. She once again shared her story and experience. Seeing so many fans of mountaineering in attendance, Phantog was very happy, saying "They are all new blood. They are so good. They represent our hope and the hope of Tibet." Today, as was Phantog's dream, there are four teams of students, mostly Tibetans, enrolled at the Tibet Mountaineering School.

Phantog with her husband and two daughters

Phantog was born in a small village near Shigatse. Her father died after she was born and the family was very poor. Her mother supported the family from only the earnings from weaving wool. At the age of six, little Phantog made a living by working as a shepherd. She wore rags but no shoes. She ate only one piece of *tsamba* a day and slept in the pen.

This was before the democratic reform in 1959. It was the fate of many serfs. In the 1950s Phantog worked on an army farm in the western suburb of Lhasa where she was selected to join the mountaineering team.

From then on Phantog devoted her life to mountaineering. She was strong and determined to succeed. In 1962, she married Deng Jiashan, a mountaineer from Wuxi in eastern China. Her husband was also appointed as headmaster of Wuxi Secondary School. Their love story during mountaineering was shot into a film called *The Top of the Goddess Peak*. The couple have now retired and have three grown-up children.

Jiji's Story

Jiji reached the summit of Mt. Qomolangma in 1999. Recalling her first experience Jiji is still greatly excited.

"At eight in the morning, we reached our goal. The sun was just above our eyes. All of us, Renna, Guisang, Tsering Dorje, Bianba Zxrasi, Luoze, Akebu, Jiabu, Laba and Tashi Tsering, made it together! We hugged each other happily on the peak and took precious photos. Then Akebu shot the video as we lifted flags and lit the torch. The mountain was covered by white snow that had been there for thousands of years. We looked towards the direction of Nepal and saw several routes but no one came up. We hugged each other, hanging prayer flags, scattering some *tsamba* into the air and praying to the Goddess of the Mountain. We shouted: 'we wish the Goddess great success!' "

Jiji, holding the Olympic torch, reached the summit of Mt. Qomolangma again in 2008.

Some of these mountain climbers have been lucky. Phantog now lives in comfort with her children and grandchildren. Some, however, were brave and strong but not so fortunate. For example, Xirao died when climbing Mount Kongur Tobe in 1961. Jiji and Guisang are still active in their work. All of them and the many others who are climbing today are threatened by cold, fear and lack of oxygen, yet none of them have ever retreated from their mission. Today, we commemorate them with honor and deep affection.

Nyima Tsering and His Mountaineering School

By Wang Ying

Nyima Tsering, the head of the mountaineering team responsible for the escort of Olympic flame to Mt. Qomolangma in May 2008, is known to many in the international mountaineering arena.

The 42-year-old Tibetan man is regarded as the "Godfather" in China's mountaineering circles. He is the founder of the Tibet Mountaineering School, one of the two professional mountaineering schools in the world. His students have become the core of Chinese mountaineering collaboration.

I met him twice. The first time was when he was descending from Mt. Qomolangma. He had tanned skin and a heavyset body, and

spoke simply and to the point. The second time I saw a more sensitive side of him. He opened a picture file, showed me a group photo of students taken 10 years ago, and he pointed to the faces of his students using a mouse.

"This is Ngawang Norbu, cameraman of the torch replay team and senior collaborator. That is Tashi Tsering. How young he was! Look at his baby face. As a cameraman, he made it to the top but then got sick. What a shame! They are all from Nielamu..."

Nielamu or Tibet Mountaineering School must be the greatest source of happiness for Nyima Tsering.

An Archer at Thirteen

"An athlete cannot be an athlete in his entire life. You have to prepare for the future," Coach Zhong Jinchang would say, when Nyima Tsering was on the Tibet Archery Team.

Tsering's hometown is Yanjing County beside the Lancang River, which is next to Deqin in Yunnan Province, and famous for the production of salt. His father died early and his mother, a doctor, lived and worked in Lhasa together with her three children. Little Nyima Tsering was naughty so his mother sent him back to his hometown where he enjoyed more freedom.

At seven, he returned to Lhasa for school. After graduation from junior high school and at the recommendation of his teacher, he joined the Tibet Archery Team.

During the following six years, Tsering developed persistence and worked hard for his future development. During his spare time, he also taught himself English.

In 1988, a joint team of Chinese, Japanese and Nepalese mountaineers reached the summit of Mt. Qomolangma. Tsering was deeply moved by the reports. He believed he possessed the stamina and strength to be a mountaineer.

He filed an application for the mountaineering team, there was no vacancy. This did not refused him. Because he was good at English, he became an interpreter and liaison officer for the Mountaineering Association. In this way he could still learn about the concepts of mountaineering.

Japanese mountaineering has great strength. Nagano Prefecture Mountaineering Association has kept friendly relations with Tibetan mountaineering circles for many years. In 1992, Nyima Tsering went to Japan to learn Japanese. He also received a deeper understanding of the international mountaineering community.

In particular, Tsering realized the importance of collaboration from the guides and mountaineers, to the service groups, the road teams and the suppliers of food. Mountaineering was not valued in Tibet so he would not have learned this if he had not traveled abroad. In foreign mountaineering missions these services, the high elevation guides, collaborators, camp service people, even the cooks were all foreigners. The Chinese mountaineering missions were in need of Chinese services.

In 1994 he visited the Alps in France and saw the success of Ecole Nationale de Ski et D'alpinisme of Chamonix, which inspired him greatly. He decided to establish a professional school for alpine services in Tibet.

Headmaster of Tibet Mountaineering School

Nyima Tsering, together with the Sports Administration, began to develop his project. In late 1997, he recruited several students from Tingri County near Mt. Qomolangma and ran a training course. It only lasted about two months, but he did not get frustrated.

The next summer, he climbed Mount Qowowuyag with Hans Schallenberger, president of OZARK of Switzerland. He spoke to him about his dream. Hans realized that here was an opportunity to promote mountaineering and his company's products in China.

He agreed to support the school annually with 150,000 *yuan* ($21,500). Now Tsering hired teachers from the Tibet Sports School, Tibet University, Tibet Medical College, the China Mountaineering Team and China Tibet Mountaineering Team. He also signed a cooperative agreement with Ecole Nationale de Ski et D'alpinisme of Chamonix, inviting French coaches to give lectures in Tibet and send two students to France for training every year.

In March 1999, Tibet Comprehensive Mountaineering Training Center opened in Nielamu. In 2001 it was renamed Tibet Mountaineering School, which is now the only other professional mountaineering school in the world, besides Ecole Nationale de Ski et D'alpinisme of Chamonix.

All students attend on scholarship which pays for tuition, room and

Nyima Tsering and Hans Schallenberger, president of OZARK of Switzerland celebrating the 10th anniversary of Tibet Mountaineering School with the torch relay team members in 2009

board, and clothing. In addition pocket money of 100 *yuan* ($14) was given every month, and they were also provided with free medical services and insurance.

His students are all Tibetans, usually from villages. For example he found four students in Nielamu, who were small but showed good physical strength and stamina. One of them, Ngawang Norbu, was such a student that he climbed Mt. Qomolangma from the north slope every year from 2002 to 2008. The last time he climbed it was to carry the Olympic flame to the Mt. Qomolangma.

However, the purpose of the school was not only to train students to become mountaineers, but also to be ones who can provide the services that mountain expeditions need, such as alpine cooks, photographers, collaborators and alpine rescuers. Tibet has many mountains, and the 10-year-old Mountaineering School quickly developed.

The school has a four-year program. Three years of studies and one year internship. To run the program the school needs to raise 15,000 *yuan* ($2,150) per student every year. The funds come from entrepreneurial patronage or earnings from commercial services that the school provides for mountaineers.

Now the school earns 700,000 *yuan* ($100,000) to 800,000 *yuan* ($114,000) per year. This income is used to maintain the infrastructure of the school, to support the Tibet Mountaineering Museum and provide rocky crags for professional training.

In the morning, teachers from Tibet University give lectures on general knowledge. Fitness classes are on Monday, Wednesday and Friday afternoons, and professional classes such as rock climbing are on Tuesday, Thursday and Saturday.

Graduates from the Tibet Mountaineering School can be seen at many important mountaineering activities. The Tibet Mountaineering Team couldn't have climbed the 14 highest mountains in the world without the support of

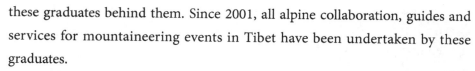

these graduates behind them. Since 2001, all alpine collaboration, guides and services for mountaineering events in Tibet have been undertaken by these graduates.

In 2003, a mountaineering event was held to celebrate the 50th anniversary of humankind's successful ascension of Mt. Qomolangma. Nyima Tsering, as the Chinese vice head of the mountaineering team, led 25 students to take charge of all alpine services, guides and photography. Tsering and five of the students also stood on top of that great mountain.

In May 2007, the State Bureau of Surveying and Mapping had a project to measure the elevation of Mt. Qomolangma. Seven students climbed to the top took charge of half of the measurements and all of the shooting. The photos for the live show on CCTV were shot by them.

Tsering has helped popularize amateur mountaineering in China as well. There are now mountaineering events and summer camps in many locations. The school also plays a positive role in alpine rescue. When an accident happens, the school is always the first to be contacted.

Value of Getting Operations Right

Tsering doesn't think highly about his achievements. Though he climbs two or three times a year, he enjoys the process and the photography more than the mountaineering. He usually gives his camera to one of his students once he gets off the mountain.

His photographs are more about the operational collaboration it takes to have successful missions. The picture he cherishes most is a group photo with dozens of his students, who stand in the dusk and look at the No. 1 camp of Mount Qowowuyag. He also shot a picture of a group of mountaineers playing golf on Mount Qowowuyag. It is this touch of the other side of mountaineering – the ordinary lives of people who come together in collaboration – that intrigues him.

A student of Tibet Mountaineering School receiving routine training for climbing

He was the only man in the mountaineering team during the Olympic torch relay to Mt. Qomolangma to carry a big camera to the peak. Taking pictures may consume energy and slow down the journey but for him beauty lies in making this effort.

As a professional and veteran mountaineer, he now has some wisdom about climbing: Work out the whole operational process before the climbing begins; Maintain a smooth tempo while climbing; Be aware that each attempt is different just like the views are different at different elevations; Passing through snowstorms safely depends on becoming close to nature.

He is always concerned about the hazards resulting from the current feverish development of mountaineering. Passion can not be the only thing in mountaineering. Sound organization should go first. High mountains are cruel and show no mercy to man. Mountaineering can only be achieved by sound and reasonable development in advance.

Olympic Torch Relay on Mt. Qomolangma

On May 8, 2008, the torch relay team of the China Mountaineering Team successfully passed the flame from the camp, which is 8,300-meters above the sea level, to the top of Mt. Qomolangma, which was a first in the history of the Olympic Games.

As vice head of the team, Tsering made sure that operations were well organized. He began preparations six months before the event was officially launched. From September 2007, members of the team went to Shenzhen and Beijing for fitness training, to Kunming for special mountaineering training and finally to Tibet for alpine training.

The team arrived at the base of Mt. Qomolangma 50 days before the torch relay. A total of 65 students from his school took part in the activity. Twenty-eight students were part of the main team including eight for the road repair team, eight for the torch team, eight for the alpine photography, and four escorts. All images of the torch relay were shot by his team members, including pictures and video clips for the Xinhua News Agency and CCTV.

Tsering is indeed the "Godfather" of mountaineering education and mountaineers. He wants to work for another 10 years before retirement. He wants to recruit international students for Tibet Mountaineering School. He also plans to expand into training professional tourist guides for the Himalayas.

Kite-flying in Lhasa

By Suoqiong & Phuntsok

When he was young, Qiangba Ngodrup, now a Tibetan doctor in Lhasa, loved flying kites. Each autumn, as a boy he helped his father dry medicine. Some medicine needs to be placed in sunlight, while others should be in moonlight. Many times Qiangba Ngodrup slept on the roof just for convenience so as soon as he woke up he could fly his kites. He knew that other children in the neighborhood could do the same thing. They were all there together, laughing and flying their kites from the roofs. Today he knows all the kite makers in Lhasa.

Following his directions, we met the Hui kite maker Anggasi in a courtyard of Tiebenggang of Barkhor Street. He is in his 50s and lives in a residential compound with his family. His house was simple and neat, just like his life.

He was just giving the finishing touches to his new kite. Anggasi spoke with us as he continued the work. He sighed that the kite business was not as good as before. In the old times in dBus neighborhood of Lhasa, there were many buyers, most of whom were youngsters.

They flew kites on roofs, squares or anywhere they could. They forgot everything else. Kite flying can be considered a regional sport for men in Lhasa. Those with scars made while kiting are proud of them.

A Tibetan boy flying his kite in 1940s

Now children have more homework and shorter vacations. Most of the land in the city is now covered by houses and highway. The kite-flying season of Lhasa has become shorter and shorter and attracts fewer and fewer people.

Anggasi believes that the Tibetan kites were introduced from central China at about the Qing Dynasty (1644-1911), but he is not sure. Probably attendants and soldiers of high commissioners brought some to Tibet from Sichuan and Yunnan provinces. The local people made improvements.

In the past, kite makers in Lhasa lived in what was known as the Jikaqi neighborhood. Many of them were of the Hui ethnic

A Tibetan boy flying his kite in 1980s

81

and came from places such as Hebalin. One of them, Shamuze, was favored by the 13th Dalai Lama, who gave him special seals and allowed him to make royal kites marked with the characters for "Fortune" or "Nine."

Tibetan kites have some unique features: First, the shapes are almost all prismatic; Second, the color is almost all white; Third, most of the patterns are about religion. For example, one pattern is the shank horn from Esoteric Buddhism, representing speed and power.

Tibetan kites have simple shapes but colorful patterns that symbolize the ethnic psychology and aesthetic orientation. In general, there are several patterns: "Jiawo" (big mustache), is a pattern that resembles a saber on both sides of the kite in red and black, representing a bold and skillful man. "Guma or Guna" (nail head or black head), has a geometric triangle on the upper side in red and black, representing the head of a guardian of Buddhism. "Miruo" (glare), has a semicircle on either side of the kite, representing a cold and hostile attitude toward the rival. "Qiwa" (gnash the teeth), has a pair of hook-shaped pattern on either side, representing the horrible teeth of a devil. "Bangdian" (apron), has stripes of all colors on the kite, representing the beautiful decorations of girls. "Galin" (shank horn), has a band in red or black on the kite, representing the power of Buddha. These patterns are simple, but they give life to the kites. When kites are flown to the sky, it is like a colorful painting. During the rest of the time some families hang the kites on the wall as a lucky token and decoration.

The season for kite flying is special. A proverb of the Han people goes like this: "It is the 3rd day of the 3rd month of the lunar calendar once again and kites will fly over the sky." It tells that a spring day with a gentle breeze is the day for flying kites.

The Hans fly kites in other seasons, but not Tibetans. In July and August of the Tibetan calendar, is the seasons in dBus, when winds were strong. It is the best time for them. People believe that if the season for flying kites comes early, then autumn will end early, and farmers and the elderly will complain.

In Lhasa, kite flying season is different. Generally kites are flown after the Shoton Festival. The kite-flying season is associated with the harvest season for farmers, so it is regulated between August and October, neither too early nor too late. Strict regulations are made about the beginning and end of the season. Some locals believe that kiting will influence the God of Wind. If kites are flown too early, the wind will come early and it will not be strong enough for the harvest season. If they are flown too late, the weather will get cold and people may become sick. So the harvest season is the best time for flying kites. At that time, the skies of Lhasa are full of kites of all shapes.

Anggasi remembers that there was a huge space behind Jiemutang. It is near the upper farmland, where farmers stock a lot of manure. Places for flying kites can be empty spaces like threshing grounds, or military training grounds. In deep fall, the sky in Tibet is particularly azure, attracting hundreds of colorful kites, like birds flying free, who are masters of the sky. Together with the high snow-capped mountains, bubbling rivers, falling leaves and flapping banners, they constitute a gorgeous picture.

Tibetans love to have kite battles. In kite season, we often can see two kites, left and right or high and low, going round and round. Soon the strings of the kites tangle. It is a competition of power between the kite fliers. The kite with broken strings will blow away, while the other kite will fly up high, winning the contest. Onlookers love to watch!

Only masters of the game know how to play well. Everybody tries to fly higher which has the advantage in the "fight" since it is easier to press the other's kite from above. The most intense time is when the strings of the "fighting" kites tangle. At that very moment, two kite fliers release string as fast as they can so that they can have the advantage and press the other down.

The result may be two kites flying away, or a fight until one falls down. If the wind is strong, and the kites flap, it is like an air raid. Actually the game is a way to show off the skills of the kite fliers.

Onlookers shout then: "If you have guts then release the kite string!!"

When a kite is cut off and blown away, eyes of all big children are glued to it. They will chase that kite like a pack of wolves running after sheep, fearing nothing at all. Sometimes with the wind, the kite will fly higher and higher.

Folklorists Phuntsok Tashi has fresh memories of this game. A lot of preparatory work needs to be done before he lets his kites fight. Generally speaking, such serious participants never buy such a kite in stores unless the makers are famous. They make their own.

The work begins with a framework. Materials should be chosen carefully. For instance, the paper for making kites should be Tibetan rice paper that is used for printing Buddhist scriptures. This paper is light but strong, so it is not easily torn by the wind. The kite should be prismatic in order to be more flexible.

The success of kite flying lies in the hands of the fliers. They control the speed and strength by releasing the string. Tibetans add *na* (glass saw tooth) to the string, which is made of powdered glass. Every kite flier has his own procedure for strengthening the string using *na*.

Some believe broken flask refills to be the best. Some say broken tea cups, while still others use glass. No matter what material, it should be smashed with a stone mortar, ground to the finest powder, and then should be boiled together with mashed rice, white sugar and a glutinous plant called "wangla". When the temperature of the mixture drops, one pours *na* onto the palm of the hand and lets the string pass through the break in the fingers.

Another man needs to stand a dozen meters away and wind the string. *Na* can be divided into three types from the roughest to the finest, whatever the kite flier wishes. The string, which is also very sharp now, may cause a careless man to bleed. However, the fun during the preparation is enough for one to forget about such small wounds.

Phuntsok Tashi said that the kind of string also plays a vital part: Rich people buy the thicker cotton made in India. Such strings can fly bigger kites and can add a wheel.

The wheel is also big and has various patterns of Buddhist symbols. Children from poor families can also make it from recycled paper, string and a tin can. Though shabby, it still is lots of fun. Children would stomp their feet on the dust to see the direction of wind. And off they go! Their laughter adds a festive atmosphere to the bustling kite-flying season.

Phuntsok Tashi recalls that only children from noble families care much about patterns and materials of kites. Each autumn they spend a huge amount of money on making good kites with the finest glass saw tooth, so that they can beat others in the kite fights.

Some rich families add a special pattern or use a particular color on a certain part of the kite, so that the kite can be easily identifiable. It seems the kite-flying season is a time for rich and noble families to show off their power and wealth.

About 30 years ago, a kite (without the wheel or cotton string) could be sold for 0.5 *yuan*, 0.2 *yuan* or 0.25 *yuan* according to the size and color. Now a white kite sells for 1 *yuan* and a colorful kite sells for 1.5 *yuan*.

Anggasi said, around 1970, his brother Yisu and he learned to make kites from an elder living in the neighborhood (who was the famous kite maker Shamuze), near the Grand Mosque. His signature of the character of "Nine" on the kite meant something then.

At Tiebenggang there is a Tibetan kite maker named Qiangba Leyxie.

His trademark is "Eight." For some time kites made by Anggasi brothers were popular. They bought a kind of paper made in another part of China. It was cheaper and strong and good for making kites.

In the peak season he can sell more than 1,000 kites. But it is no longer enough to make a living. Anggasi sits and smokes at his kite booth, watching people coming and going. He is like a statue standing in the river of time, without making a sound, or heaving a sigh. A little bit like the kites that wait for the next puff of wind to take them again dancing into the wind.

Meeting with Maigelong of Ngari

By Li Xiaolin

Early in the 1980s, when the Qinghai-Tibet Railway was still under construction, there was a saying that goes: "It's easy to go abroad but difficult to reach Tibet." But you may not know that it is even harder to reach Ngari when you are in Tibet. I have been to Ngari twice. Maigelong! I will remember you in my entire life!

In September 1999, I went to Ngari from Lhasa by car on the new Xinjiang-Tibet Highway that runs between the Himalayas and the Gangdise Mountains. We drove day and night and reached the Pulan (Burung) County of Ngari Prefecture three days later.

This was the first time I visited Ngari. I was keenly aware of what it meant to be in the "vast and magnificent" land of Tibet.

In September, 2006, I visited Ngari again, driving from Yecheng in Xinjiang to the town of Shiquanhe. It was from the opposite direction but it still took me about three days.

In Ngari, there is a very great living Buddha of the Bon religion, a Tibetan medicine master well-known in Tibetan-inhabited areas. His name is Tenzin

Wangta. Adults and children, monks and ordinary folks in Ngari honor him by calling him "Maigelong," meaning respectable elder and living Buddha.

Maigelong was an important and irreplaceable figure of Ngari's intangible cultural heritage. Only he can deeply understand the history and traditional culture of Ngari, especially about Shangshung civilization and the Bon religion. If we compare Shangshung civilization and the Bon religion to a lock, then one of the keys to that lock is in the hands of this elder.

During my two visits to Ngari, I was very lucky to see him twice.

1999: In Shiquanhe Town

Maigelong's home was Shiquanhe. He lived in a common courtyard home between buildings of Tibetan Medicine Hospital. His two-story building had flapping banners, golden Dharma-cakra and two bronze fawns on the roof. Inside the small courtyard solar panels resembling satellite receivers were erected among colorful plants.

That first afternoon, the directors of Tibetan Medicine Hospital and an interpreter brought me to his home. I presented him with a *hada*. I also delivered Tibetan herbs produced by a private enterprise in central China and a pharmaceutical plant in Tibet—two big boxes of painkiller pastes and a boxful of herbal granules.

An amiable and kind person in an old washed-out crimson frock was my first impression of Maigelong. The elder first presented me with a *hada*, a box of saffron and a bag of Tibetan medicine.

Tibetan people believe that their medicine, made from the raw materials from sacred mountains and lakes, can cure many diseases. Maigelong said that such medicine has a substantial role in their religion. When I left Shiquanhe, he gave me a book written in Tibetan about astronomy, calendric calculations and the Bon religion. It was like the ancient books and scriptures often seen in a monastery. In the book, Maigelong wrote about his beliefs and understanding about religion and life about our senses, reality and the ideal. What should people do when they are still alive? How should we spend our lives?

Maigelong giving some medicine to his patients

Two Tibetan women came to see him. They first presented him a *hada* and bowed to him, half kneeling down in front of his seat in the process. Maigelong was very patient. He inquired about nature of the disease. He carefully observed the tongue and felt the pulse. Then he prescribed the medicine to suit the illness.

Maigelong would meet patients and guests in a small room. The Tibetan wooden cupboards and walls in the room were covered with photos. They were taken in different places—postcards with the background of Potala Palace, Jokhang Temple, and photos of former President Jiang Zemin meeting with Tibetan doctors. The bookshelf was full of Tibetan classics, including his book *Ancient History of Ngari*. One could feel the pulse of history by touching these books printed on long strips of Tibetan paper with ancient printing techniques.

The district Tibetan Medicine Hospital was rebuilt after the reform of the 1980s. There are now more than 200 doctors in the region. Maigelong, 78, had worked 37 years in the Tibetan Medicine Hospital.

"When President Jiang Zemin visited the Tibetan Medicine Hospital in Lhasa, I suggested he increase the number of doctors in Ngari and now we have this new building. All my life sticks to the principle of serving the people wholeheartedly. I helped some and was rewarded a lot. I determined to bring up capable people and push forward Tibetan medicine. I know a little about the ethnic cultural tradition. I hope to hand my knowledge down to the future generations," he smiled. He paused from time to time to discuss with the interpreter how to better convey his ideas.

Recently, Maigelong is particular pleased that Hebei Province has offered an assistance fund of 4 million *yuan* ($571,000). The autonomous region has allocated 1.5 million *yuan* ($215,000) to build a new outpatient building and inpatient department at Ngari. The building will be magnificent, complete with Tibetan traditional architectural features. It will be the best and most beautiful building in Ngari. Religious motifs, including the golden roof and Dharma-cakra of the building, have been designed exactly to the elder's specifications.

He spoke to the people in charge: "This will be the Tibetan Medicine Hospital, not an office building of some department."

With most of his dreams fulfilled, he now worries about the actions of irresponsible, profit-motivated individual enterprises which have had negative impacts on Tibetan medicine. Tibetan herbs in today's market are not as good as before. Even speaking about these dissatisfactions, he was still calm. Nothing could ripple the deep water of his heart.

Maigelong's living habits have been a concern. Rumors say that he almost never sleeps on his bed but sits cross-legged in the scripture hall. I asked him about it. He only sleeps four or five hours every day and eats only one meal at 1:30 in the afternoon. His meal is some *tsamba*, cheese and butter tea. Sometimes he will have some Chinese cabbage. He never has any sugar and won't touch meat at all. He drinks a lot of butter tea, at least one flask (a five-lb. container) a day. Maigelong is in good physical condition. Except for catching cold occasionally, he never suffers from any other diseases. He lives a regular life. He almost never watches TV, answers telephones or goes to the park. He chants scriptures when he has time.

There is a group photo of Maigelong and Kong Fansen, the former Party

secretary of Ngari, placed conspicuously on the cupboard beside the bed. They were good friends and had a lot in common. These years, Maigelong always misses Kong,

"Although I am a believer of Bon religion while Kong was an official of the Communist Party, we shared a lot in common. For example, the idea of that we should help people find happiness of the Bon religion and the idea of serving the people wholeheartedly!"

"What is the relationship between Tibetan medicine and religion?" I asked.

"They both belong to the traditional Tibetan culture. Tibetan medicine employs special means and herbs to diagnose and treat people. Chanting scriptures, praying and other religious rituals provide mental reaction and psychotherapy. For patients, presenting *hada*, paying money, bringing some *tsamba*, lowering their head to touch that of a Tibetan doctor are ways to express their wishes. These acts cannot cure diseases directly, but the patients feel happy when they do so. From a mental perspective, it helps treat the diseases and we should make use of both."

Tibetan Buddhism and the Bon religion have the same ideas with different names and forms.

"As a faith, they are equal. But the forms and teachings are totally different." Maigelong made a metaphor: "The water of Brahmaputra, Lhasa and Shiquanhe are the same for easing thirst and watering plants. The water is the same, but the names of the rivers are different."

"How has the Bon religion influenced on Tibetan medicine in Ngari?" I wanted to know.

Among the classics of Bon, there is a special one on Tibetan medicine, astronomy and calendric calculation. As a living Buddha of Bon, Maigelong holds religious rituals that are somewhat different in detail with those of Tibetan Buddhism. The content of the scriptures are almost the same.

He said: "Some patients go to see Tibetan doctors or lamas because they follow the rituals of Tibetan Buddhism. But we all cure patients. We all follow the requirements under *The Four Medical Tantras*. Chadrel Rinpoche and Soru Tselan, two respectable masters of Tibetan medicine, follow the tradition of Tibetan medicine as I do. The difference is that I am not as good as they are."

Tibetan medicine is so vast and deep as a sea. Maigelong believed that it started thousands of years ago. It would be difficult to bring all the *The Four Medical Tantras* into practice.

"What we now can master and employ is only 10 percent to 30 percent of the whole. Things would be better if we could make use of 50 percent. It needs thorough study to fully understand and practice it."

The elder continued, "During the Cultural Revolution, I was forbidden to work as a doctor, but lots of patients came to see me secretly at night. Later the restrictions were lifted. Then I set a rule that I wouldn't charge anything for my medical services. People thought much of me and would always send me *tsamba* and put money in the bags of *tsamba*. I never thought to take anything from my patients. I just wanted to help them relieve their pains and not fail their trust!"

He never spent any of the money patients gave him on himself. Instead he gave it all to the Tibetan Medicine Hospital and to do good deeds. When he came to this point, he smiled like a child.

In November, 1997, Maigelong was invited to Switzerland. He brought Tibetan herbs worth 10,000 *yuan* ($1,500) from the pharmaceutical factory of the autonomous region and gave them to Tibetan people and members of the Tibetan Medicine Association in overseas countries. Since then the Swiss have supported his efforts.

He made a pilgrimage tour to India and Nepal and visited Beijing. But he has never been to the ruins of the Guge Kingdom in Tsada County, Ngari

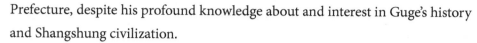

Prefecture, despite his profound knowledge about and interest in Guge's history and Shangshung civilization.

Maigelong thinks that the opening of his Tibetan Medicine School in the Gangdise Mountains conforms to Deng Xiaoping's economic theory. The requirements for the school enrollment were very specifically to enroll orphans or children of poor families.

The elder said: "Though these children may not have sound background, they will do much good for the society, the county and the people!"

He only can go to the school once or twice a year. Every time he goes, he gives every child a *hada* and 10 *yuan*. He speaks highly of the Swiss who volunteer to teach in the school.

We visited his scripture hall and pharmacy upstairs. On the walls of the scripture hall hang Thangka of Sakyamuni and Master Zongkapa, as well as Yotok Yonten Kongpo, a Tibetan saint of medicine. There are 12 Thangka

Maigelong reading in the scripture hall

depicting the history of Bon and the story of the founder of Bon and his apprentices.

Maigelong sat in the scripture hall, demonstrating the ritual of beating the sheepskin drum. He allowed me to take pictures. Every night, he sits cross-legged here. On the shelf against the wall are books, scriptures and artifacts, as well as over 20 national, regional and prefectural-level honorary certificates. In addition to being a national role model of ethnic unity in 1988 and 1994, Maigelong was elected member of the 8th National Committee of CPPCC.

Classics are not the only books in the scripture hall. Counting those in the Gurujiang Monastery and Tibetan Medicine Hospital, he has at least 15,000 books. There were more before the Cultural Revolution but many were destroyed. Some of them are rare editions brought from India. Over 300 are about Tibetan medicine.

On the opposite of the scripture hall is a hospital pharmacy. There are three large, tall wooden boxes full of Tibetan herbs, more than 150 kinds in total. Ngari has poor natural conditions and ecological environment. As a result, herbs are not widely distributed. When Tibetan Medicine Hospital processes these precious herbs, Maigelong and several old Tibetan doctors will chant scriptures as a way of protection.

Directors of the Ngari Tibetan Medicine Hospital and I roughly estimate that starting from the democratic reform of 1959, which redistributed land and reorganized the political structure of Tibet, so far Maigelong has treated more than 200,000 patients, including Tibetans, Mongolians, Hans, Huis and some foreigners.

Before the democratic reform, Shiquanhe was a wasteland. It had been set as the prefectural capital and become over-populated. The ancient tamarisks were cut down, leading to soil and water loss. Recently, China has made investments and replanted the tamarisk trees so that people now finally realized the irreplaceable role of this beautiful plant.

It will take some time to restore the capital to its former beauty. The newly-planted trees are about six feet high, but that will come in time. Now they stood along the streets of Shiquanhe Town tossing away their leaves in the winds of fall as we said goodbye.

Since I left Ngari, Shiquanhe's tamarisks and of course Maigelong have often come to my mind. They both connect with my heart.

2006: In Gurujiang Monastery

In September 2006, we visited Maigelong at his Gurujiang Monastery. After a long and difficult journey, we picked up an interpreter, Dawa Drolma, in the town of Menshi.

Dawa Drolma is a graduate of Southwestern University of Finance and Economics. Her hometown and Maigelong's are both in Nagchu and she speaks the Amdo dialect of Tibetan. The woman was quite modest, saying upfront that she had no knowledge of ancient Shangshung civilization and profound Tibetan medicine, but in fact she was very helpful.

Menshi is 13 kilometers away from Gurujiang Monastery. The land is flat and grassy with abundant water and so good for farming and herding. At present, the barley was ripe so the vast area was a golden sea. Farmers were busy happily harvesting, packing and transporting. The bumper crop added to the sense of harmony and vitality. A bubbling blue water river flowed to the southwest. It is the upper reaches of Xiangquan River. Except for pilgrimage and Tibetan patients, visitors seldom come here.

Believers of Bon say that Gurujiang Monastery on Khyunglung Zongkar Mountain has had a Bon ashram for at least two or three thousand years. The earliest gymnosophist Jampa Ramgar, though not the greatest living Buddha of Bon, was quite influential here.

The meditation cave at the hillside is called Gyungdrung Rinchen

Gyungdrung Rinchen Chabu, the meditation cave at the hillside

Chabu (Holy Cave). Seventy years ago, a great living Buddha built Gurujiang Monastery with the cave at its center. The major buildings of the monastery include four or five hallswith statues of the founder of Bon made of gold, silver, bronze, stone and clay. Of course, there are also pagodas, artifacts, Thangka and scriptures.

The most precious ancient book is the *Bon Tripitaka*, as well as teachings of its founder. There are also commentaries written by the later generations. Master Jampa Ramgar, the founder of the Gyungdrung Rinchen meditation cave, was believed to be not just a prince of the Kingdom of Shangshung, but also reincarnation of a wise man named Gshenrab Miwoqie.

The faithful believe that he lived for 3,000 years and accomplished 12 great deeds, winning thousands of believers. This is how the Bon religion spread. In addition, his youngest brother, Guru Rinpoche Padmasambhava, is the one who Tibetan people respect the most. Followers of the Nyingma school regard him as the second Buddha. At that time, Bon spread throughout Shangshung. In the Tubo period, it became influential among the royal family of Tibet. Today it has an influence in the daily life of all Tibetans.

For the past five years, Maigelong has been meditating at Gurujiang Monastery. We followed a winding pathway up the slope of the mountain, climbed stone steps and wooden ladders, and entered the mystic meditation cave.

The cave was a hall of about 10 square meters. Except for a small space for practicing meditation, the place is full of Thangka, *hadas*, Buddhist images and butter-burning lamps. Leaning against the rear wall were neatly placed scriptures, including Maigelong's new work *Collections on the Culture of Shangshung*. The walls of the cave were blackened by the smoke of butter-burning lamps over the centuries. The solemn atmosphere filled in the small space in a way that encourages contemplation.

I presented my book that included my interview with him. Unexpectedly he was particularly excited and pleased by *Tree of Wishes in the Snow Land—*

Studying Buddhism at the meditation cave

Tibetan Medicine and Tibetan Herbs. I was moved by this. He kept reading the book, joyfully pointing out group photos of him and his apprentices. Later, he put the book on the shelf by the window, together with those profound classic works. It made me feel glorious as well as a bit humbled.

Now 85, Maigelong looked healthy and energetic, and smiled a lot. His normal routine was to get up at 3 o'clock every morning, chant scriptures and meditate, and then sleep at 11 o'clock at night. He sits and sleeps. It is a simple way of life. His meals still consist of butter tea, *tsamba* and a little yogurt and cheese, and on occasion some Chinese cabbage.

In the past decades, every October to the next March, Maigelong retreats to this cave alone to practice meditation. However, even at such a special time, he still spares three hours from 1 to 4 pm to see patients. During the breaks, he only leaves himself five minutes to have some *tsamba*.

The retreat is most important for a monk. Nothing should disturb it. Nonetheless, he believes that curing patients and saving a life is also a high-level practice.

At the foot of the mountain there are only two or three herdsmen families. The biggest building is the hospital that was built three years ago. It is the key medical project supported by the prefecture and county health bureaus. There were six inpatients.

Everyday, Maigelong sees from 5-10 or even 50-60 patients. Most of them visit the holy mountains before they come to see him for medical service. Some patients suffering backache and rheumatism were there. I realized that this was more than a patient-doctor relationship. This was also a relationship of faith between believers and a living Buddha.

There are four apprentices here from Ngari. In summer they learn Tibetan medicine theory and pick herbs on the mountains; in winter they study Bon and Buddhism. Another apprentice, Kelmad Jiangcun, in his 30s, has spent more than 10 years learning about Shangshung civilization from his master. He

has since been sent to Lhasa to study computer, modern science and culture.

At dusk, Maigelong, holding a crutch, walked down from the cave. He gave us some introductory material on Shangshung culture. He suggested that we could discuss it the next day in the cave. The golden light of the setting sun spread over the vast land and covered the elder in his white hat and crimson frock. He pointed to the desolate ruins on the mountain on the left side of the monastery. This is all that remains of the Shangshung Kingdom's legendary capital Khyungpo Sengchen and the palace where the three kings of Shangshung once lived.

The ancient Shangshung Kingdom was divided into upper, middle and lower parts. This area was in the upper part and it was topped with the castles of the 18 tribes of ancient Shangshung. It was in these mountains and rivers that the Shangshung civilization came into being, developed, flourished and faded away.

Later on I learned that it was also a hub for many kinds of religions and civilizations. Two thousand years ago, the Greek historian Herodotus wrote in his famous work *History* about Ngari. The kingdom was thought to be rich in gold. In the 1720s, headed by Portuguese priest An Ruite, Catholic priests disguised as businessmen went to Ngari, and established the first Catholic Church in Tibet. However, their efforts were in vain.

The spread of Bon and the role of Shangshung characters in Tibetan writing demonstrate the role the unique and colorful Shangshung culture played in the history of Tibetan civilization. Young lamas of Gurujiang Monastery often take out the old almanac which shows a clear record and history of Bon beginning thousands of years ago.

Then came Buddhism which took the place of Bon to become the mainstream religion for Tibetan people. The once flourishing Shangshung civilization left tremendous mysteries for the later generations to unlock. Perhaps Maigelong is a channel connecting the past and the present here.

The next morning, as the sun rose and the moon still hung in the sky, we visited the meditation cave again. Sunlight penetrated from the small window on the wall, covering the body of Maigelong and creating some indistinct flashy halos. Just like the visit in Shiquanhe Town seven years ago, as a master of religion, the elder sought nothing from me but I, as an ordinary mortal, was eager to seek out answers to numerous questions. I had plenty of questions to ask, some of which had haunted me for quite some time.

As a living Buddha and a Tibetan doctor, Maigelong has multiple identities and roles to play. Some come to him for his superb medical skills, while others come for religious guidance. Others come with both. Which identity did he care for the most?

"I am a living Buddha. My job is religion, but I practice medical service as well. I started to study Tibetan history and culture and medicine at the age of six. When I was 20, my mentor died and made me as his successor.

"After the peaceful liberation of Tibet, the government hoped to make full use of my knowledge and skill so I mainly practiced medicine. I also spent a lot of time and energy studying Shangshung culture and Bon religion as well."

"Which one is more satisfactory among these roles?" I asked.

"Ngari is where I provide medical services and where the function of Tibetan medicine can be best used. It is the real and true service for the people. However, I may have greater and wider influence in terms of religion."

"What aspirations do you have?"

"I have exerted great energy in the prefectural pharmaceutical factory. Now it is built, but it still needs money for modern equipment. Tibetan herbs are good and inexpensive and people need them. I worry about this. Because of insufficient funding, the factory is sometimes idle.

"I hope you, as well as other reporters from Beijing, can help me get further support from the government. I have also asked the local government to establish a cooperative medical service across the counties and villages of

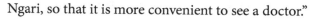

Ngari, so that it is more convenient to see a doctor."

"What will the future of the Bon religion be like?"

"In Ngari, there is only one monastery, namely Gurujiang Monastery, that is Bon. There are not many believers. However, more and more people in the Tibetan-inhabited areas now have a greater interest in it. Some foreigners do research on the Bon religion as well. So the number of believers is increasing. The Bon religion has a close relationship with Shangshung civilization. I have confidence in the development of both."

"How do the rich and the poor get along and maintain the harmony of the society?"

"Compared with the past, most of us are not poor any more. So the poor people need to be calm and keep their minds peaceful. Some people do live a wretched life, but the government has provided them many preferential policies and support. The rich, on the other hand, should show their mercy and contribute to society. In the end, I believe that Tibetan lives will get better."

"After substantial improvement in living conditions, how do people improve their spiritual life?"

"Nowadays a lot need to be done in terms of the spiritual world of people. Lust and desire have grown to enchant people's inner depths. In the ideal and perfect world, everyone lives with compassion, mercy, love, and peace in mind. But, Gurujiang Monastery was not built in a day."

"Where do you want to go in the future?"

"Twenty years ago, the Tibetan Medicine Hospital of the autonomous region asked me to go to Lhasa, I didn't agree. I am old. I don't want to go anywhere. Ngari falls behind other places and it needs me more. Though I grow old, I still treat patients whenever they come to me. Sometimes I have to visit their homes to see dying patients. In a word, I am bounded to this land."

After saying goodbye to the elder, I stood in front of the meditation cave and looked out into the distance. The water in Xiangquan River was flowing downstream. People and livestock could be seen in the distant vale. It was peaceable, just as it must have been, for so many thousands of years before.

Forever: Appreciation and Best Wishes

During both visits, he was so considerate of me that I felt at ease. He never "taught" me directly, however, his words melted the ice in my heart. He was like the sun in autumn on the highland, giving warmth and peace to the innermost parts of my heart. How I wished I could forever stay in such sunlight with Maigelong and listen to him, or just stay with him without doing anything. This was a time of happiness for me.

I remember the first time I came back to Beijing from Ngari I happened to read *Tristes Tropiques* by Claude Lévi-Strauss, about his experience in the Amazon jungle.

He said, "When places where civilization does not perish or become merely a distant memory but instead continues to be something very real, it is possible to come across truly very original and special people. You can not imagine such encounters. You have to hope that someday you will have one."

Maigelong was just such a human being I realized, from my close encounter and experience on the plateau.

One day in late autumn of 2007, I received an e-mail from Dawa Drolma, the interpreter from Menshi. Maigelong died!

Did my master, my dear friend, the successor of Shangshung civilization who had enlightened me, the great living Buddha of the Bon religion that infused me with hope for the future really, truly and veritably leave the world? I am not a wish-maker, but I had made a wish I could visit Maigelong some day again. But now, my wish will never be more than that!

Maigelong! I will remember you in my entire life!

The New Bards of Tibet

By Yang Enhong

Many excellent ballad singers such as Zaba, Tsewang Jugmi, Adadhar, Khaca Zaba, Anqin Dorje and Drolma Laktse, have passed away in recent years. Who will carry on the art and oral tradition of ballad singing? Many ballad singers are illiterate. What a loss if such masterpieces like *The Epic of King Gesar* were lost for good.

The Epic of King Gesar is a 1,000-year-old work and the longest epic in the world. It tells the story of Gesar, the superhuman warrior ruler of the Kingdom of Ling who waged war with the nearby Kingdom of Hor and relieved the suffering of the poor.

Darwa Zaba, a "Divinely Chosen" Artist

Most of the young bards begin this way, have dreams as a child and when they wake up, they begin to perform *Gesar*. The dreams mostly have several major themes, such as seeing King Gesar; seeing a man in white riding a white horse; being asked to choose things; being asked to "read" or "eat" the tome of

103

The Epic of King Gesar.

The dream of 28-year-old artist Darwa Zaba is the most typical. He was born in Moyun Town, Zadoi County of Yushu. He had a dream when he was 13 years old: He was asked by an old monk in the dream to select one from three things, the language of flying birds, the language of running beasts, or the ability to sing the story of Gesar. He thought that others might not believe him even if he could understand the language of animals. So he selected *The Epic of King Gesar* and then he was able to sing the legendary story.

When he was about 16 years old, he had another dream – a man in white riding a white horse took him to King Gesar. The rider, Ludrup, was from the dragon world and the representation of the previous life of Nacha Adeng, Uncle Caotong's son.

In the dream, he was taken to a big tent and met the sacred King Gesar. He wanted to offer sacrifice to King Gesar, but he had brought nothing. So

he used all kind of deeds he had done in the previous and the present lives and offered them as tribute. He also saw a number of tents, fresh flowers and armored warriors. Darwa Zaba was told he was the representation of Nacha Adeng.

Darwa Zaba fell ill for three days and nights after returning home. After he had recovered, he went to the mountain. He saw the mountain and waters of Ling, which made him so excited he wanted to cry. Then he began performing "Chapter of the Heaven" from *The Epic of King Gesar* then other chapters like "Chapter of Birth" and "Horling."

Between the ages of 13 and 17, he often went to the mountains in secret and sang the stories there. No one knew about his singing. He began to feel uncomfortable when he was not singing.

At 17, he made a pilgrimage to Lhasa. He passed Nagchu on the way and met another balladeer. When the artist performed the first chapter of "Horling," Darwa Zaba joined him and performed. He sang for about five hours.

He returned to his hotel in Xiachokha. That very night Darwa Zaba started to perform the epic in a dream. The performance lasted till the noon of the next day. When he woke up he saw many people looking at him from his door and windows.

The news that Darwa Zaba was able to sing *The Epic of King Gesar* spread quickly. From 1996 he worked at the Yushu People's Art Center. He could perform 170 chapters. Nineteen chapters have been recorded so far, three have been consolidated and one published.

Nowadays, Darwa Zaba and his parents live in Gyegu Town. He is a contract worker in a government office, and earns 1,700 *yuan* ($242) per month. He lives a modern life, drives his car and dresses like any other young man, but he still has the stories of Gesar coming endlessly to his mind.

In 2003, he was invited to perform at the Fifth International Symposium of

Darwa Zaba, an excellent ballad singer performing *The Epic of King Gesar*

The Epic of King Gesar to celebrate the 1,000th anniversary of this masterpiece. He was admired by all the attending scholars. He also went to Beijing in the summer of 2005 and agreed to be interviewed for this article.

Darwa Zaba never attended school. He memorizes and then records this epic. When he is performing, he puts all of his energy into it and forgets everything else. It is difficult to interrupt his performance with words.

Though he believes that the stories of Gesar come to mind at the inspiration of the gods, he does not deny that he once heard the performance of his uncle, who was also a bard. When it comes to his version of the "Battle of Horling," it is shorter than that of Zaba, his uncle.

He said, "Generally speaking there are three kinds of performance: long, short and medium. Before the performance, the singer asks for God's decree to sing the long one or the short one.

"Take 'Zhuguguo Zong' for example, the long version requires 200 tapes to record it. The longest stories include 'Zhuguguo Zong,' 'Battle of Horling' and 'Mengguma Zong.' 'Battle of Horling' can be as long as 250 tapes, or as short as three or four tapes. Generally a singer will not perform the short version if he believes that will be harmful to his life, as it is believed to be a sign of disrespect for King Gesar.

His cousin Sonja is one-year younger than Darwa Zaba. He is a ballad singer as well in Zadoi County. Unlike his cousin, he feels free to control his performances.

Sita Dorje from Zaba's Hometown

The geographical and cultural environments of the balladeers are part of the Tibetan traditional culture and influence the performances. There are new bards ready to sing the epic ballads that are Tibet's most beloved work of art. Most of the artists come from remote pastoral areas, or at the source of the three big rivers, the Yangtze, the Yellow and the Lancang rivers. The singers of Golog Tibetan Autonomous Prefecture in Qinghai come from counties of Madoi, Gade, Jigzhi and Baima, all of which are remote areas at the source of the Yellow River; Sita Dorje is from Zaba's hometown, Palbar County of Chamdo of Tibet, a place that has little transportation. The artists from Nagchu Prefecture were born in the remote pastoral area of Nagchu County, while some others were born in Shantsa, Palgon, Dirl and Amdo counties far from Nagchu Town. Their performances are part of the heritage of Tibet and the unique rules of the oral tradition of *The Epic of King Gesar*.

The older artists had their particular way of singing *The Epic of King Gesar*. The performing styles, contents and

Sita Dorje, the youngest ballad singer, from Palbar County, Chamdo

stories have been passed along to these younger artists. In this way they carry on the traditional performing style of the epic. People can still tell the influences of the older artists by watering the younger ones.

Sita Dorje, the youngest, at 17, from Palbar County is an example. He was born in the hometown of the famous Zaba, so when people discovered his talents, they called him Artist Zaba. Though he has never met Zaba, his performing style and tunes are extremely similar to his traditional performing style.

The difference was that he, too can sing freely. Before he starts to perform, he envisions the scene first. When there is a stop, he is also able to stop right away. The older artists, such as Zaba and Sandrol, however, could rarely be interrupted once they began.

As Zaba puts it, "Singing *The Epic of King Gesar* is very sacrosanct, it would be disrespectful to King Gesar if the singer stops in the middle of a paragraph.

Sita Dorje sings clearly, has a large vocabulary and a bit of a local shading accent. Though he carries forward the tradition, he still adds his own characteristics. For instance, he divides each chapter of the battles into two parts. According to him, the first part is about the battle and the second is about the trophy.

He has chapters of his own style, such as "Battle of Nangling" and "King of Sibuta." According to him, Chamdo people don't like singing or listening to the first part of "Battle of Horling," while Nagchu people don't like singing or listening to the second part of "Battle of Horling." It is because in the first part, the Kingdom of Hor invades the Kingdom of Ling, killing Caotong's son and Jiacha, taking away Qomu, so Khampa people believe that it is ominous. While Nagchu is the place where the Kingdom of Hor used to be, so in the second part the Kingdom of Ling defeats the Kingdom of Hor, and Nagchu people feel ashamed to sing or hear the story.

A strange dream drove Sita Dorje to perform *The Epic of King Gesar*. The dream is quite similar to that of the old artist Zaba.

"It was when I attended my primary school in Shading. One night I slept in the dorm after class. I had a dream that I roamed around and got to a place of mountains, water, flowers, grasses and cows. Two tall horsemen came up, wearing armor. I was much afraid.

"They came to me, dismounted their horses and introduced themselves. One of them called himself Xinba, while the other was Danma. Xinba gave me a *hada* and said: 'King Gesar asked us to bring back someone for him, and you are that someone.'

"So I was taken to a place beside a big white tent. I looked down and saw many people and tents.

"Xinba spoke to King Gesar who sat in the tent, 'We have brought the person you want.'

"King Gesar said, 'Today is a good day.'

"I saw many books there. King Gesar gave me a book and said: 'Eat it up.'

"I was afraid and thought, 'How can I eat a book'? Danma put the book into my mouth.

"King Gesar said, 'On this good day, you will ascend to Heaven!'

"Then he turned his back to me. Suddenly a rainbow appeared before my eyes and flew away as I stepped just one foot on it. When I woke up, I didn't know where I was. I found myself in the dorm. I thought for a while and the horse rider and the words on the book appeared before my eyes. I walked out of the dorm to a table-tennis table. I sat on it and kept feeling how strange the dream was! The scenes of the dream kept coming before my eyes. I felt choked with so much weight on my chest.

"At breakfast, my classmates ate, but I was full and had no appetite. During the first class, I couldn't focus myself on the lesson. The scenes of the dream kept coming back to me. I felt so strange. The classmates said I was not like before.

"The second class was a music lesson. I couldn't hold it in any more. I said to a classmate that I want to say something. Sonam Qunsok, the music teacher, said: 'Go ahead.'

"So I went up and sang. while I was performing, the scenes of the dream and words on the book came before my eyes. The teacher said: 'You are telling the story of Gesar!'

"I asked: 'What is Gesar?'

"Then I thought, *so they were the stories of Gesar*! My heart was filled with awe. Since then, I can tell the stories of Gesar at any time."

Sita Dorje said he had never listened to the story of Gesar before. But, in his hometown of Reba, an old man used to tell stories about Gesar. He and his friends often gave something to the old man and asked him to tell stories of Agu Dengba, as well as folk stories like *Rock Fat and Mouse*. He still remembers him. It may require further investigation and study to unveil the mystery of how Sita Dorje was infused with stories of Gesar. Despite his denial of his contact with the stories of Gesar, Palbar County, his hometown, indeed is a place where these have spread wide and far. His interest in Tibetan folk literature and edification of folk literature may be important factors of his ability to perform *The Epic of King Gesar*.

When I interviewed Sita Dorje in October 2006, he was a third grade student at Palbar County Middle School. In 2007, he passed the entrance exam to Chamdo Middle School and began high school.

Young Bards at Gesar Performance Hall

In the past, artists who made their living performing *The Epic of King Gesar* had no social status. They wandered about the highland to gain a living. They followed pilgrims and caravans and sing *The Epic of King Gesar* in

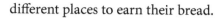

different places to earn their bread.

This is the way that a number of excellent ballad singers were brought up. They were endowed with broad minds by the imposing mountains and waters on the highland. They enriched and polished their performing styles and techniques by meeting with artists from different places. Most of the outstanding ballad singers led a life of wandering and singing.

The younger artists today live in a new society. Though they have a stable life in the countryside, they are attracted by the modern life in the cities. They use more convenient transportation and sing *The Epic of King Gesar* in a modern way.

Nagchu Town of Tibet is an example. In the mid-1980s, the People's Art Center of Nagchu Cultural Administration first established a Gesar performance hall (Sgrung Khang), in which performances are staged at a fixed time and place and by a certain artist.

The audience can listen to the performance for half a day for one or two *yuan*. This form of singing *The Epic of King Gesar* developed and became commercialized. Now in Nagchu Town there are three privately-run Gesar performance halls. The owner hires ballad singers to give performances every morning and afternoon and pays them a monthly salary of 300-800 *yuan* ($42-114).

The audience will not only listen to the *The Epic of King Gesar*, but also will spend money on tea and meals. Attracted by this, young artists come from remote hometowns to Nagchu Town and can find a permanent employment. They can rent a house and start a life of performing *The Epic of King Gesar* in the cities and townships.

At present, a dozen of young artists live in Nagchu Town. Most of these artists give performance of *The Epic of King Gesar* while some sing in other places and do some other business as well. For instance, artist Tashi Dorje from Nagchu County is not only a singer but also a doctor. He built a house in

Nagchu Town and settled there.

The earliest dweller to Nagchu was Tsering Zhandui who settled down in Nagchu from Shantsa County in 1987. Now he has become a staff at the People's Art Center of Nagchu Cultural Administration, taking charge of organizing and managing ballad singers. Another Nagchu artist, Pekar, also lives in Nagchu, and works for the People's Art Center.

This experience in performing and the wider range of opportunities to carry on contact and exchanges with other artists enable them to become more skillful. In this way the Gesar Performance Hall in Nagchu Town has attracted more and more ballad singers, making it a real communication and exchange center for *The Epic of King Gesar*.

In the 1980s, a large-scale rescue and promotion campaign of *The Epic of King Gesar* has helped improve the social status of ballad singers. Gesar culture has become a pillar in the social life and spiritual world for people in pasturelands. Under such atmosphere, a young generation of people under the influence of *The Epic of King Gesar* has grown up.

In addition to the influences by television, newspapers and books, the spread of the Tibetan opera of *The Epic of King Gesar* and establishment of facilities for Gesar culture have exerted a positive impact on those young people. So this new generation of balladeers will become the generation that carries forward the ethnic traditional culture of Tibet.

The Father and Son Photographers in Tibet

By Suoqiong, Wan Jing & Lin Min

In the 1930s, Demu Tanzin Gyatso, a living Buddha in Lhasa, challenged the tradition and embraced the new. He recorded the changes of Tibet through his lens, turning a new page in the history of the remote and mysterious region. His son, Demu Wangjiu Dorje, went on to capture Tibet with this same deep grasp of his people and their land.

Demu Tanzin Gyatso

Demu Tanzin Gyatso, was a member of the upper class of Tibet. He was the honored 9th Living Buddha Demu of Tengyeling Monastery in Lhasa, as well as one of the four major Khutuktus (living Buddhas) recognized by the imperial court of the Qing Dynasty (1644-1911).

In the fall of 1912, an European tourist wanted to take a photo of Demu who was at that time only 13 years old. The young boy grew restless after sitting on his chair so long because of the slow speed of the camera or the dim light in the hall. The photographer then asked the lamas around to bind him on his chair so he could take the picture.

In Tibet, nobody dares to bind a living Buddha, who usually enjoys great respect among the people. Therefore, all the monks were terrified.

The palace administrator thought that the foreigner was insulting the living Buddha intentionally and decided to drive him away from the monastery. The European made vain attempts to explain his idea. Later, the living Buddha Demu felt it a pity he had no photo of himself when he was young.

In the 1920s, a Nepalese opened a photo studio in Lhasa that attracted Demu. Most people believed that their souls would be sucked out by this fancy machine and dared not to have their picture taken. The photographer couldn't sustain his business and then became seriously ill.

The living Buddha Demu showed great mercy to this poor Nepalese and tried to save him. The photographer was moved by this and decided to give his set of British-made Caybin cameras to the living Buddha as a gift before he died.

The living Buddha started to take pictures. He shot many photos in Lhasa and Gongbo, his hometown. His photos provide a window to the world to understand the society, traditional culture and lives of monks and nobles of Tibet.

He set up his own darkroom for developing and printing, and bought equipment for enlarging photos. Using top-grade foreign-made cameras, such as Caybin, Leica and Chase, he shot a large number of pictures. He had his own improvisational style.

Tibet was blocked off from the world and quite conservative at that time. Only occasionally would someone casually mention foreign scientific findings. Photography was considered to be an evil "witchcraft," which would take people's soul and bring disaster to them.

Even as a living Buddha, Demu could not take photos freely. Once he secretly took pictures of a large important religious festival in Lhasa. He was found by the security lama who gave chase but couldn't catch him.

Though the local people were very conservative, they showed great interest when they saw the pictures. Gradually, other nobles and rich families in Tibet followed suit, buying cameras from foreign countries. Nobles took pictures when they visited one another. In this way photography became a fashion.

In 1951, when Tibet was peacefully liberated, Demu Tanzin opened the granary to assist the People's Liberation Army. He then became the member of the editorial committee of the Tibetan Military Region and executive director of Tibet Branch of the Chinese Buddhism Association.

His works covered a wide range of subjects according to Demu Wangjiu Dorje, his son and a renowned photographer in his own right. Many of them however were destroyed during the Cultural Revolution and only 300 pictures remain.

Demu Wangjiu Dorje

During the 3rd International Photographic Art Exhibition held in Beijing in 1985, a photo named "Spring in the Ancient Temple" won first prize, making the author Wangjiu Dorje famous overnight. The gold prize was a recognition of his understanding of life and the times, and it thrilled him all the way in the deepest recess of his heart.

To Wangjiu Dorje, success was all about the right timing of his shutter. A simple device like a camera will bring out different results in the hands of different people. In the hands of Wangjiu Dorje, the lens of his camera becomes a pair of honest eyes, observing Tibet all the time.

Wangjiu Dorje, also known as Demu Wangjiu Dorje, is the son of Demu Tanzin. Born in December 1949 in Lhasa, he began working in 1969. He is now vice-chairman of the Tibetan Photographers Association, member of the Standing Committee of the Tibet Committee of the People's Political Consultative Conference and a visiting professor of the Art College of Tibet University. His photographic works *Eagle of the Snowy Mountain* and *Rider* have won second and third places in Tibetan and national contests. He also won the Fuda Cup Awards for the "Exhibition of Photographical Works in 40 Years of China." Sixteen of his art works, including *Mounted Archer, Cremation* and *The Master* have won dozens of international, continental and national awards. In 1999, Wangjiu Dorje was honored as a member with "Moral and Artistic Qualities" by the China Photographers Association.

A Hobby Inherited from His Father

In 1956, Wangjiu Dorje got his first camera, a small one which his father bought him as a gift. The first photograph he took was of his own house which was under renovation. His father gave freedom to his son to photograph without giving too much direction or criticisms. He only reminded his son to have an idea in advance when taking a picture.

When he was a middle school student, Wangjiu Dorje continued to show interest in photography. In 1965, the Exhibition Hall of Tibet was under preparation and needed help. The project manager asked the assistance of the Lhasa Middle School.

During the work, Wangjiu met some photographers. Under their guidance, his passion for photography grew. He shot photos of the school sports meets and the surrounding community.

The greatest wish of Wangjiu Dorje was to become a professional photographer. However, while he was still in middle school, the Cultural Revolution took place and crushed his dream. During the Cultural Revolution, he and his family were accused and tormented. After it ended, the regional government held a grand mourning ceremony for his father, who had died from illness.

Wangjiu Dorje's wish was finally fulfilled. He went to work for the Tibet Federation of Literary and Art Circles and was assigned to the newly established Tibet Branch of China Photographers Association. His dream of becoming a photographer came true.

Snapshots of Spring in the Ancient Temple

One day in March 1984, monks of Tashilunpo Monastery paid a visit to Shigatse. Wangjiu Dorje and his colleagues planned to take some photos of the life of the lamas. When they got there, lamas were still chanting Buddhist scriptures in the hall. So they waited outside. About one hour passed and the lamas came out in a huge crowd. So they started to shoot. After taking a few pictures, however, Wangjiu Dorje felt that something was missing, but he could not tell what exactly it was. At that moment several lamas walked out a few steps in front of the crowd. These lamas standing out in front were just then lit up by a beam of sunlight, which made their cloaks and caps shine like gold.

Wangjiu Dorje's heart beat fast: That was it! He seized the moment, held his camera steadily, pressed down the shutter and made the shot. *Spring in the Ancient Temple*, the gold-prize winner, came into being. Even today Wangjiu Dorje is still tremendously excited about it.

For him, after an arduous process of seeking, he found what he wanted by sheer luck. It took merely one 60th of a second to catch that shot. He had indeed been through tough times and twists and turns, but that one photograph was the effect of his persistence to awaken his dreams.

A picture reflecting the daily life of lamas, *Spring in the Ancient Temple* also provides an image mirroring the spiritual world of lamas and their religious activities. It also reflectes China's policy of religious freedom. The different ethnic peoples, occupations and experience may hold diverse understanding of what culture is and draw varied and even opposite conclusions of its artistic values. To Wangjiu Dorje, however, it was just a relief from the debt of gratitude he felt, as he finally presented the yesterday, today and tomorrow of a people who had brought him up, to the rest of the world.

It was perhaps the award winning *Spring in the Ancient Temple* that triggered the surge of popularity of realism photography in China. In the days that followed, the fates and living conditions of ordinary people became the focus of the lens of photographers.

"Personal Tibet" in Lens

Someone asked Wangjiu Dorje what was the greatest fun in life for him. The answer was "the moment I press the shutter." He wants to record the real Tibet, his "Personal Tibet," on camera. The prize winner *The Master* was completed in 1983, when the reform and opening up of the 1980s were adopted in China, inspiring people of different nationalities in the snow-capped plateau.

The picture shows a large group of people, old and young, smiling to their heart's content. Wangjiu Dorje captured this historical moment echoing people's feelings. During his career he drove to and visited places across dBus, gTsang and Khampa of the eastern Tibet, capturing the beauty of the mountains and rivers of Tibet as well as local folk customs.

He likes to take pictures of ordinary but distinctive figures of Tibet because he can "read the eyes of people brought up by this land." When he runs out of inspiration he turns to a stack of his bad works and loses himself in them.

What was wrong in these photos? Wangjiu Dorje would start afresh and examine himself. It was due to this kind of self-examination that he realized the difference between him and his father. He saw from the relatively fewer pictures taken by his father that they were too pragmatic for him. Photos taken by his father were not intended for anything. He was just shooting photographs to be a mirror of the old Tibet.

After studying his father's works, Wangjiu Dorje realized that his father lived in a more peaceful place, which enabled him to develop his photography to take pictures for that won prizes .

Such a pragmatic or intentional approach could ruin a good photographer. From the photos taken by his father, Wangjiu Dorje saw the need for a different person, a different role as a photographer. Tibet, in which he dwelled, also needs to change. Recording Tibet through the lens became the starting point for Wangjiu Dorje.

The difference lies in the eyes of the people in the pictures. He can read the eyes of people who have made their homes in this land. Wangjiu Dorje through his own lens in his head, records the states of mind, the living conditions and the changes in people of the present. He wants to be sure that he has captured something that is real. Only then, can it deserve to be photography.

The father was the first photographer of Tibet, who left images reminding people of the yesterday. The son is a photographer of the new generation, who provides pictures for today and tomorrow.

A Tibetan Author Writes About the Tibet He Knows

By Ling Shijiang

Published by the Ethnic Publishing House in 1999, *Souls on the Strings* is a collection of short stories written in Tibetan by Tashi Bandian. A bestseller in Tibetan-inhabited areas in southwest China, the book reflects the lives of local people.

The author thinks that literary works should be rooted in the real history, literature and cultural dynamics of Tibet. It should reflect the ongoing huge changes that Tibetans are experiencing. It is the task of writers to keenly understand the pulse of the times.

"This is the tenets of my work. I believe that writing in my mother tongue is conducive to the understanding among my people who are kind, lovely and respectable," he says.

Tashi Bandian was born in 1962 into a farmer's family in Ranba Village, Rinpung County of Shigatse, which is 300 kilometers west of Lhasa. He is the second of six children. His parents saved every penny to support his schooling in Rinpung County Middle School.

Being a good boy, Tashi Bandian joined the labor team after school to help relieve the family's burden. His teacher liked this diligent student and encouraged him to develop a good command of Tibetan and literature by reading more books. Sometimes the teacher gave him additional assistance to improve his skill.

During the Culture Revolution millions of students dropped out of school. Tashi Bandian had to quit his school in mid-1970s as well. He still longed for knowledge.

One day he heard that a city-educated young man had arrived in his village, bringing some Tibetan books with him. Tashi Bandian dared himself to ask if he could borrow some books from him. They later became good friends. His new friend encouraged Tashi to improve his education through reading.

After a day of hard work, Tashi would read using the oil lamp until midnight. Worrying about his eyesight and cherishing the lamp oil, his mother asked him to go to sleep earlier; but his father supported his son's choice.

"Reading makes a person wise, just as the Buddhist doctrine does. We are poor, but knowledge will bring us fortune," said Tashi to his parents.

One day the father and the son went into mountains to collect firewood. The snow-capped mountains aroused the interest of the young boy: What does the outside world look like?

He asked his father, "Where is Lhasa?"

121

"It is right on the other side of those mountains," replied his father. "Look, the far end is the Nyainqentanglha Mountain Range. A mountaineer needs courage to climb atop the mountain. Diligence is the path to the mountain of knowledge."

That night, Tashi wrote down a few lines in his diary, "Work hard and embrace the world outside the mountains." Later he would write a prose titled *I Look Away* to express such feelings, which was later adopted into the Tibetan textbook for middle school students.

An opportunity came when the village needed a new Tibetan teacher. Tashi, who could now read and write, was selected. The salary for a village teacher was low but it provided stable income for him to support his family and to buy more books.

Besides teaching and farming during the day, he continued studying in the evening.

For the following eight years, he read Tibetan literature as well as world literature. Such self-taught experience laid a solid foundation for his career as a writer in the future.

In May 1983, Tashi Bandian was invited to Lhasa to attend a writers training course. To get there first he walked all day to Padang District. The second day he went across the Brahmaputra River to Nyemo County and finally caught a long-distance bus to Lhasa. The one-month training was fruitful for Tashi, who said later that only after taking that course did he understand how to write a story.

In the mid-1980s, a new system greatly raised the enthusiasm of local farmers in Rinpung County and their income rose consequently. Witnessing such changes, Tashi decided to write a novel about them. In 1991, *Days in the Lives of Ordinary People* was completed after he made six drafts.

With multiple characters and a twisting storyline, the story is about the

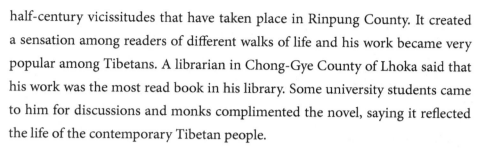

half-century vicissitudes that have taken place in Rinpung County. It created a sensation among readers of different walks of life and his work became very popular among Tibetans. A librarian in Chong-Gye County of Lhoka said that his work was the most read book in his library. Some university students came to him for discussions and monks complimented the novel, saying it reflected the life of the contemporary Tibetan people.

Torla Nicholas, a young French professor of Oriental Languages School of the Sorbonne, who had spent a long time at the Tibetan Academy of Social Sciences, spoke highly of it, "This is the real picture of the life of contemporary Tibetan people." He brought the book to Paris and shared it with students studying Tibetan culture to show them an example of Tibetan literature.

Nicholas visited Tashi often. As time passed, they became good friends. Since 1997, when Tashi graduated from the "Intermediate Correspondence Course of American English," they were able to communicate with each other both in Tibetan and English. Nicholas read other works written by Tashi Bandian as well, such as *Tomorrow Will Have a Finer Weather* (1985) and his 1999 novella collection *Souls on the Strings*.

Tashi continues to write and has expanded his writing into poetry, prose, literature criticism and reporting. He became a member of the Chinese Writers Association. He won first prize of the first Tibetan Literature Awards of Five Provinces and Autonomous Regions in 1985; the "Belle-Letter Prize" from the Chinese Literature Foundation in 1994; the second "Qomolangma" Literature and Arts Award in 1995 by the Tibet Autonomous Region; and an award from the first "Gangjian Cup" Tibetan Literature Awards in 1996. He was given a "Self-Taught Award" by the All-China Federation of Trade Unions and elected one of the Top 10 Outstanding Youths by the Tibet Autonomous Region.

Now Tashi Bandian works as an editor of the Economics Department of

Tibet Daily. Apart from work, he continues to write stories. Recently, an article in "Culture News" talked about the flourishing of Tibetan literature and ranked him the top writer of those who write in the mother tongue.

Some people who have only visited Tibet once or twice write fancy stories about the region, but actually their stories are far from the real Tibet. Tashi Bandian believes that the best way for a writer to depict the true Tibet is to live with the local people just as he has done for so many years.

Doing Well by Doing Good

By Raymond Zhou

Dawa is the founder, president and chairman of the Tibet Dashi Group, with diverse businesses in water resources, road construction, tourism, and other industries. But his most outstanding product is premium cooking oil, which he markets under the brand name, "Tibet Nature."

Dawa is expanding now, and is open to all possibilities, including joint ventures and foreign investment. Eventually, he wants to market his products internationally. He is confident that he can do it because the Tibet Dashi Group has the unique advantage of products created on the roof of the world — Tibet — and nobody else has that edge.

Dawa Dondop has two wardrobes: At home he often appears in traditional Tibetan garb, sitting in his spacious living room furnished with authentic Tibetan decor, sipping butter tea, or looking from his balcony onto the Potala Palace just a few streets to the south.

In his office just around the corner, he prefers a white shirt with a warm-colored tie, talking with vendors or clients with the eloquence, cosmopolitan flair and sophistication to match any big-league businessman in a major city.

Whatever his exterior, Dawa has the imposing physique of a Khams man from eastern Tibet and the self-confidence to go with it. That may have helped make him an emerging star in the Tibetan business world.

"The walnut oil we produce comes from wild walnuts that grow on trees 3,700 meters above sea level. Some are 100 years or older. They are truly one of a kind. Our standard rapeseed oil also contains 46 percent walnut oil and the Tibetan variety has 51 percent, compared to 37 percent for the top brands produced in the rest of the country. Only a few Canadian brands can match our quality," the 46-year-old entrepreneur says.

Oil from Snowy Regions

When the Qinghai-Tibet Railway opened in 2006, the very first freight train carried 4.14 million *yuan* ($636,000) worth of "Tibet Nature" cooking oil to Shanghai. Dawa has since relied on the rail line for shipping. "It saves us 70 percent in transport costs compared with trucks, which is crucial for a low-value-added agricultural product," he explains.

Shipping by train takes 18 days to reach major destinations like Beijing, Shanghai and Guangzhou, a bit slower than by truck. But it is more reliable and each shipment has at the most two to three damaged cartons, much fewer than when shipped by truck. Trucks often travel over rough roads, and sometimes roll over, causing much higher financial losses.

Dawa has two very different strategies for rapeseed oil and walnut oil. The Tibet Nature Agriculture Co., the arm of the group in charge of producing and marketing cooking oil, has one-seventh of the 70 million *yuan* ($10.8 million) Tibetan market for rapeseed oil, with a 5-10 percent profit margin.

"I'm not going to take it nationwide because I cannot make much money out of it. But I'm not giving it up either because 200,000 Tibetan farmers benefit from it, directly or indirectly," says Dawa.

For walnut and healing oils, which can reportedly lower cholesterol, the profit margin can be as high as 30 percent. Retail prices doubled from 2004 to 2005, turning the product into a cash cow with even greater potential. "And 300,000 farmers from seven Tibetan counties form our supply chain," he notes.

Dawa would not reveal financial details, but said "Tibet Nature" broke even in 2006 and revenues have been doubling year by year. Group-wide profit has grown 15 to 20 percent annually.

Trustworthiness

With so many suppliers, mostly home-based, management is tricky. When Dawa first started, he learned the hard way what it's like to deal with people who do not know what a contract entails.

In 2003, he signed contracts with seven county governments to buy 26 million tons of rapeseed. Soon after, market prices rose and farmers sold their yield to higher bidders. Local governments did nothing to deter them. As a consequence, Dawa lost five to six million *yuan*.

"You cannot blame anybody. People, including government officials, did not have a sense of abiding by a contract. Creditworthiness is important, but it's only possible when all sides follow the rules," he said.

In 2005, he went a step further and dealt directly with village committees. That year, the rate of contract fulfillment reached 50 percent. It was also around the time that governments at higher levels invested four million *yuan* ($615,000) to develop 45,000 *mu* (about 3,000 hectares) for high-quality

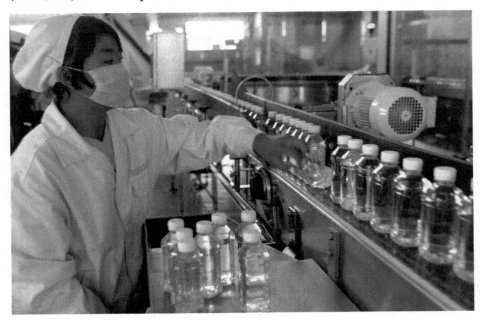

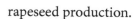

rapeseed production.

Dawa has been the largest buyer, and to set a good standard, he pays a small premium while guaranteeing a floor price and letting it tick upward as dictated by the market.

"Now, rapeseed farmers beg me when harvest season comes, but I shoulder the biggest risk in price fluctuations."

Between doing well and doing good, Dawa never lets one eclipse the other. When he contracted for the job of upgrading the Sichuan-Tibet highway in the late 1990s, he hired an engineer, who twice demanded surcharges after the contract was signed. "In the end, I did not make a penny from the project, but I guaranteed our work was top-notch," he sighs with relief.

In business as in life, there can be blessings in disguise. When Dawa quit his first business in late 1980s, he sold his truck to a man in Lanzhou. But instead of paying him the promised 33,000 *yuan*, the buyer could only pay an initial 12,000. While waiting for him to come up with the remainder, which took six months, he put himself up in a cheap hotel in Lanzhou and there met his future employer-partner, who accepted Dawa's truck resale debt as equity and took him to the Pearl River Delta.

Building a Business, Brick by Brick

Dawa's resume as an entrepreneur is so full of adventures that any part of it can be sketched out in colorful detail. After returning from southern China, he ran a "mobile business" involved in border trade. He also spent the year of 1992 in Hong Kong selling a Tibetan herbal medicine. While there, he noticed that many of the business empires were family based.

"Someday, I'll have a big company named after me," he thought. Hence was born "Dashi", a Romanization of the first syllable of his name (*shi* in Chinese means family).

Dawa believes in investing in the future. In 2003, he spent 75 million *yuan* ($11.5 million) on state-of-the-art equipment from Sweden that ensures the best quality of processing.

He also credits the government aid that tided him over several difficult transitions. But according to Wei Sanxing, an official with the Tibet Enterprise Union, a trade organization, some central government subsidies for the distribution of agricultural products do not reach the grassroots level. "You see the money is there, but there are barriers to prevent you from obtaining it," he explains.

"The government has a lot of preferential policies for us. But getting handouts is like catching fish. The most important thing for us to learn is fishing," adds Dawa.

He is now concentrating his efforts on building a distribution network in the coastal region.

"We have won quality certificates from Germany and Japan as well as from our own country. We have a big market in quality-conscious metropolises and all we need is a sales channel that best positions our products and reaches our clientele," says Dawa.

In Shanghai, he is talking with a big food company for an equity partnership. In Beijing, he hopes to set up boutiques and rent counters in upscale department stores.

"We are putting in our own money now, but we're open to all possibilities, including joint ventures and foreign investment. Eventually, I'll take our products to the international market. I know I can do it."

Outlook

Dawa is aware that the bigger his business, the more he'll be held up as a model by the government as well as by his compatriots. "Tibet does not have hi-tech," he says. "All we can provide is the value of agricultural products. I'm a farmer's son and I'm also a Buddhist. Being religious means to do good things for others."

Dawa says that the Tibetan history of mixing religion with politics has acted to curb people's business sense. Tibetans who are in business often do not have enough confidence, he says, especially to keep up with rapid changes.

"Tibetan Buddhism emphasizes reincarnation. I tell my sales people that when you sell one *yuan* of goods, you're actually committing ten cents to the happiness of your afterlife because you have made it possible to raise the living standard for others. But if you make one *yuan* by evil means, you're adding ten cents to your record of evil, for which you'll be punished in the next life," he says. "Doing well and doing good overlap here, and you no longer need to burn incense and say prayers every day."

A Distinguished Professor at Tibet University

By Duoqiong & Penpa Tsering

Changngopa Tseyang graduated from the Central University for Nationalities in Beijing in 1975. She had a dream to be a journalist, her first choice was not teaching. Nonetheless it has become her lifelong career. Being a teacher has brought her great honor and respect both from her students and from scholars around the world.

She said: "I cried when I was assigned to teach in Tibet Teachers' College. I was so reluctant at that time. Now when I look back after 20 years, being a teacher turned out to be the best choice for me."

A Family with Education Tradition

Tseyang was born into a noble family, that had produced several influential figures in Tibetan history. In the early 1740s, Changngopa Namso Taj was the doctor of the 5th Dalai Lama and a noted scholar and educator. He was mentioned many times in the autobiography of that Dalai Lama. Under his direction Namso Taj moved the Tibetan Medicine School from

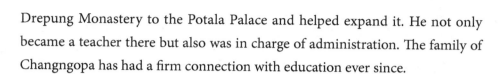

Drepung Monastery to the Potala Palace and helped expand it. He not only became a teacher there but also was in charge of administration. The family of Changngopa has had a firm connection with education ever since.

When the 13th Dalai Lama introduced new measures into Tibet, he selected four young and brilliant people and sent them to study advanced science and technology in the United Kingdom. The youngest and most talented among them was from the Changngopa family. Changngopa Rigdzin Dorje was also the grandfather of Tseyang.

In 1925 after Rigdzin Dorje finished his study and returned, he designed and built Tibet's first electric-power generator in the Duodi section of Lhasa. He was project designer as well as educator in this capacity. He had a particular capacity for teaching his workers and staff so that they could fully support the project. The generator started generating electricity two years later.

Her father, Changngopa Dorje Ngodrup was a pioneer in translating new textbooks into Tibetan. He later assumed the office of the vice director of the Department of Education of Tibet Autonomous Region.

Her father encouraged her to teach at the Tibet Teachers' College, saying, "Teaching is a good occupation for you. What are you waiting for? Go for it, we will fully support you."

As a college teacher, she first taught translation theory. Today she is a professor of Tibetan history at the Department of Tibetology, Tibet University and works as a visiting professor at Sichuan University.

Tseyang is an excellent teacher. Her 1999 history majors honored her with a *hada* which reads, "Good teachers, whose love toward education is as deep as the sea, have students around the world." She showed us the bundle of letters from her students who have become the backbone of different departments and businesses.

From Ordinary Teacher to Tibetologist

Tseyang has become a world-renowned Tibetologist, whose motto is "No teaching, no research."

"Thanks to the reform in the 1980s and cultural exchanges with other countries, my research has gained recognition among my international peers. This also widened my own vision of study."

In early 1999, Tseyang became the first female professor of Tibetan history at Tibet University as well as the only female supervisor of master candidates. Her first thesis "Discrimination of the Name of Samye Kloster" won second prize of the first academic symposium of Tibet University in 1985.

Since then, Tseyang has become more intensely interested in Tibetan Studies. In 1985, her paper "On New Policies and Administrative Measures of the 13th Dalai Lama" was read at the National Seminar on Tibetology held in Wenjiang. She delved into many archives and interviewed many people, when she was writing the paper. Her work attracted wide attention and has been cited by many experts.

Tseyang's research was regarded as a forgotten corner by Tibetologists. When it comes to research of the lineage of Dalai, researchers usually pay more attention to the achievements and contributions of the 5th Dalai Lama, but she focused on the lives of the 3th and the 4th Dalai Lamas.

Apart from teaching, Tseyang often visited Potala Palace to read scriptures and historical materials. She consulted many elders to gather firsthand information. Based on the field investigation, she wrote a number of papers that have drawn attention from domestic and overseas Tibetologists.

These papers include "Investigation of the 3th Dalai Lama Sonam Gyatso" and "Investigation into the Track Record of the 4th Dalai Lama Yonten Gyatso." Some of them have become precious historical archives since some of the elders she interviewed have passed away.

In 1992, together with a noted scholar Donggar Lobsang Trinley, she attended the Sixth International Association of Tibetan Studies held in Norway. She read her paper "Investigation into the Track Record of the 4th Dalai Lama Yonten Gyatso" which was one of the selected papers of the conference. The paper for the first time revealed that the 4th Dalai Lama Yonten Gyatso had his enthronement in Drepung Monastery instead of Reting Kloster. It cleared away the doubts and misinterpretation about enthronement of the 4th Dalai Lama, arousing interests among international Tibetologists.

A noted Japanese Tibetologist told Tseyang: "I have been thinking about writing about the 4th Dalai Lama and you showed me the way. Thank you."

Many foreign Tibetologists asked her: "You have done a lot in Tibetan Studies. Where did you begin your education?" They were surprised to learn that she studied in Beijing and that many of her teachers were Han people.

At every International Association of Tibetan Studies, Tseyang attends as a member of the Chinese Delegation of Tibetological Studies and presents and publishes her research findings. Many foreign institutions of Tibetan Studies and universities have sent her invitations to cooperate and lecture.

She was invited to the Center for Advanced Study of the Norway National Academy of Sciences, from November 1995 to June 1996, as a visiting scholar. She was part of a cooperative research program on the Bon Tripitaka *Gangyur*. She not only gained a leap in her Tibetan Studies but also improved her English proficiency and computer skills.

In 1979, Tseyang went onto further education at the Central University for Nationalities. She enrolled in a two-year study of ancient Tibetan, which laid a solid foundation for her future study.

In 1999, she participated in a conference on Women's Studies at the University of Oslo as a guest scholar. She also was invited by the mayor of Chicago to a grand millennium celebration featuring 100 famous people across the globe. In 2000, she attended a seminar of the International Union of Anthropological and Ethnological

Tseyang (center) with her colleagues

Sciences held in Beijing and Hong Kong, and to a seminar on Development of the West Regions and Tibetan Studies. In 2001, she was invited to the UK-hosted International Association of Tibetan Studies.

Celebrating Tibetan Women

Recently Changngopa Tseyang has been researching the subject of Tibetan women and has published many papers. Tseyang attributes this to her students, "I owe my new work to my students. They have many enlightened ideas."

One student asked Tseyang a question that no one had ever raised: in the history of Tibet classes the role of women in her Tibetan history is not mentioned. The question brought her to think deeply and urged her to start Tibetan Women's Studies.

She found that Tibetan women have made great contributions to Tibetan civilization and development. From 1989 to 2001, she wrote several papers, including "The Life and Story of Trimolu, Queen of the Tubo Empire," "Tibetan Women and Traditional Education," "The Role of Women of the Upper Classes in Traditional Education" and read these papers at the 7th, 8th and 9th International Association of Tibetan Studies held in Austria, US and the Netherlands. She was also invited to institutions of higher learning and academic institutions in the UK and France.

In "The Life and Story of Trimalo, Queen of Tubo Empire" she demonstrates that this brilliant Tibetan woman played an important matchmaker's role in the marriage between Princess Jincheng of the Tang Dynasty and Tesenpo Tride Tsugtsen of Tubo. In her papers, she put forward several academic viewpoints that no one had ever voiced before.

She said, since the old Tibet was a society of feudal serfdom, there were clear rules and regulations. Women had no right to participate in the management of state affairs, and intelligent and smart women were disparaged.

Despite this, there were many brilliant and strong Tibetan women, noble and otherwise, who did heavy household chores well and were responsible for the education of the children.

She said: "My mother is a good example. She is the daughter of the nobleman Zhandong Jumei Gyatso. She went to school when she was very young and traveled to India. She spoke good English and Tibetan, and a little Chinese. She taught me how to read and write."

To attract more research on Tibetan women and encourage Tibetan young women, at present Tseyang is busy with preparations for the Research Center on Tibetan Women at Tibet University. It will be the first research institute on Tibetan women in China.

Daughter, Wife, Mother and Friend

As a teacher, Tseyang has many students; as a Tibetan researcher, she has made great academic contributions; and she is also a good wife and mother. Many may take it for granted that given her achievements, Tseyang would have little time to do homemaking.

"I am good at cooking Western dishes. My parents, husband and child love my cooking. Whenever I have time, I like to cook for my family and friends," she said.

Her husband Cilang, a computer engineer, works in Tibet's telecommunications department. When their child was young, Cilang often traveled on business. So she took care of her child by herself. Now her parents grow old, so she also looks after them.

Tseyang's only daughter studies at Tibetan Middle School in Beijing. She's lively, active and likes to play football.

"My daughter is in junior high school in Beijing. Sometimes I miss her so much, I am sad and I feel depressed. But as soon as I step into classroom and see my students, I am full of energy.

"Nowadays students have many channels to gain knowledge. They do not rely merely on teaching materials. They also have higher expectations of their teachers. A teacher must read extensively and keep abreast of new ideas and breakthroughs. This way we can be a useful guide for our students."

Besides historical books, Tseyang likes to read classics from home and abroad. Her room is full of books and magazines, ranging from the latest issue of *Life* magazine, to literary books like *A Dream of Red Mansions* and *The Red and the Black*. Her desktop and laptop computer are her best friend.

Besides reading, Tseyang likes listening to music and singing. She loves American country music the most. She frequently joins parties at school and with friends, often until the wee hours of the morning. She says that these too are forms of communication and learning.

Tseyang likes making friends also. She observed, "Sincerity comes first when making friends with others." With a young and sincere heart, she has

many bosom friends, no matter whether they are Tibetan, Han, or people from abroad.

Tseyang always says, "I sincerely thank my teachers. They led my ship into the sea of knowledge and guided me in my pursuit of the starry sky."

Marriage of Phuntsok

By Yuqian & Jin Yong

Surrounded by huge mountains, Tare Village lies in the far north of Rinpung County of Shigatse on the northern shore of the Brahmaputra River which passes through the lower part of the village. A little nunnery stands on the small hill in the eastern part of the village. Nuns there are daughters of the families of the village. When no ceremonies are held in the nunnery, they live in their own homes like other girls. There is a hot spring under the cliff at the western end of the village where villagers, men and women, bathe from time to time. Tare Village, which is home to more than 500 villagers in 50 families, is divided into upper and lower parts; there are no roads connecting it with surrounding villages. Villagers begin work at dawn and rest at dusk, leading a simple traditional lifestyle.

I have visited Tare Village several times to film a documentary and have become familiar with the villagers. When they see me, both adults and children rush to me, asking me for photos.

Once, I visited the village to attend the Ongkor (Bumper Harvest) Festival. Moreover, a young villager named Phuntsok entrusted me with the task of persuading his father to allow him to get married in Lhasa. We got off the bus at Yade Bridge, which is the nearest stop to the village, and waited for Phuntsok's family to pick us up.

Yade Bridge used to be a dock, where villagers along the river gathered. However, from time to time accidents took place due to the deep and narrow water. In 1995, local government built a bridge, providing the convenience for people across the river.

There is a small two-room stone-built store by the road. It looks tiny, but it has long been a point connecting several neighboring villages. This is the only way for people to cross the river or leave the mountain. Everyone goes there, drinking sweet tea or wine made from highland barley. The shop has a telephone. When those working away from the villages want to reach their families, they have to call here, trusting the owner of the shop to ask passers-by to pass the message on to the family.

Phuntsok

Phuntsok is an old friend of mine. I first met him when I was taking a course in the Tibetan language in Lhasa Kungshan Language School. Phuntsok, being a newcomer to Lhasa, was only 19 years old then. He worked in Kungshan, cleaning, providing security and teaching the Tibetan language

and earned a salary of 400 *yuan* ($55).

Once, while Phuntsok was on leave from the school, the water was cut off, so people left the water faucet on. The next day, he got to school and found out that the first floor had been flooded and some goods were damaged. The merchants demanded compensation from the school which then demanded that Phuntsok pay.

At that time, Phuntsok was not self-confident. He couldn't defend himself, so the school deducted it from his salary. Even that was not enough, and Phuntsok brought another 2,000 *yuan* ($285) from home for the compensation. Even then the school wouldn't let the matter rest and demanded a further deduction of two months' salary. When he saw me, Phuntsok told me about the matter and he couldn't help crying, repeating, "What if the school gives me the sack?" His concern was that the school would fire him after deducting all his salary.

Later I got familiar with Phuntsok. I gradually learned about him and his

Phuntsok's "grandma"

Phuntsok's father

hometown, which caught my interest.

There are 11 members in Phuntsok's family. He has two sisters. The elder sister, Gezong, married two brothers in Nakartse County of Lhoka. Life after marriage was hard for her as the brothers would often beat her. The younger sister was seriously ill at the age of 14, so she became a nun in the nunnery after she recovered. She stayed home all the time to help her mother with house chores, except on the 10th, 15th, 20th and 30th days of the month in the Tibetan calendar when she would go back to the nunnery to chant scriptures.

Among the six boys, the eldest son, Phuntsok, and the third son, Namgye, worked in Lhasa. The second son, Gonggar, was at home with the farm work. Phuntsok's uncle, Ngodrup, has no sons, so he adopted Phuntok's fourth brother. The fifth son, Gyatso, and the sixth son, Tashi, were still in school. The youngest sister, Yeshe, a very cute girl, was in junior grade in the township middle school.

Phuntsok's mother

Phuntsok's sister

Phuntsok's father used to be a teacher in the town's primary school. He took charge of the family after retirement. Phuntsok's mother, an industrious and frugal lady, is 43 years old this year. She is not in good health. In Phuntsok's family, there was a "mola" (grandma). In fact, she was not the children's grandma but an aunt. Since her parents died early, she took the responsibility as a parent and brought up her two brothers. Her little brother died early, but the elder brother, Phuntsok's father, got married. In this family, her brother and nephews showed great respect for her and called her "Grandma."

Tibetan Wedding Customs

The vast and arid Qinghai-Tibet Plateau has a small population. Marriage customs in the region vary from place to place, based on local situations. Generally speaking marriage takes several forms: monogamy, polyandry, and other arrangements such as a person taking the spouse of his or her dead siblings. Among these forms, monogamy is quite popular and polyandry is also widely accepted.

In a family, men are the pillar and the future. The property and social status of a family always depends on the number of men. The brothers of the family sharing one wife centralizes the means of production and allows a sound division of the labor force. For example, if a family has three men, the wife will take care of the household chores, and the eldest son will manage the whole family and make major decisions. The second son will go out working and bring back information from the outside world. The third son will go herding and do farm work. In such a way, the family will accumulate wealth and not be easily bullied, so it will become prosperous quickly. In Tare Village, most families follow this mode.

Being a mountainous village, Tare Village has few means of transport. It takes at least three hours for the villagers to leave the county by horse. Lands around Tare Village are not very fertile and the major crops are highland barley, wheat, potatoes and cole. The village is half cultivated and half pasture. Though it is located in the mountains and on the river, local people still find it hard to get firewood and water. The fuel is cow dung and bushes cut from hills, which requires a lot of labor. It takes half a day for local people to fetch a barrel of water, so they prefer using ponds during the rainy seasons. In 1998, local government initiated the "Mother Earth" project, drawing up spring from neighboring mountains to Tare Village.

Phuntsok's second younger brother, Gonggar, received no schooling because the family lacked manpower. Though illiterate, Gonggar was good at farming and even tailoring. Gonggar got up early and got to bed late, but he could never finish the farm work. Phuntsok, according to his parents' arrangement, went to school for formal education, to prepare to become a qualified "patriarch."

According to tradition, as the eldest son Phuntsok will be the patriarch of the family after his father passes away. For boys in the mountains it is lucky to be appointed "patriarch" by their parents, which means that the boy will have absolute authority in the family and will receive respect from the family and others.

Phuntsok's parents had a wish that their six sons would marry one wife so that the family would remain unified. So after Phuntsok graduated from junior middle school, his parents let him become engaged and decided to hold the wedding ceremony in winter.

By custom parents decide when and whom their children will marry. Parents will tell their daughter one day before her wedding. The boy will know that he is engaged but nothing about his bride. The couple are supposed to meet the very night of the wedding ceremony. This tradition has been passed down for generations.

Phuntsok passed the entrance exam to the senior high school of the county, but his father asked him to leave the school and to get married. Phuntsok then wished to work in Lhasa, but his parents did not agree. They feared that the son would "go bad and against his parents' will" like other villagers who changed after going to Lhasa to work.

The Runaway Bride

A month before the wedding, the bride suddenly ran away and the wedding had to be canceled.

I met the runaway bride in Lhasa and learned about the story. The girl, named Tendron and now living in Pusong Town of Rinpung County, has a brother. Her mother died early and her father married with a girl almost the same age as the daughter. So the atmosphere of the family grew a bit odd. On the day of the engagement, Tendron was sent by her father to the home of some relatives. When she returned, she found many presents in the house. Her father told her that they were given by relatives. She was so glad and tried on some new clothes and ate a lot of candies.

A week before the wedding, when Tendron was returning from the fields, she heard girls gossiping about her engagement. She then understood what those new clothes and cakes were for. That very night she overheard the conversation between her father and the stepmother, learning that she would soon get married. Tendron said girls in her hometown had great fear about marriage because families would not let daughters know anything before the marriage. All of a sudden that a girl has to go to a strange family and live with several men. Girls with good luck will meet good men while those less lucky will live with alcoholic and even violent husbands.

Tendron didn't know Phuntsok and his brothers, let alone their appearances and characters. She had just heard from friends that Tare Village was very poor and had no road at all. She didn't want to go to that place, so she fled secretly to Lhasa. She found a friend of her mother's and worked there as a babysitter.

Phuntsok's father, a stubborn man, was keen on face-saving. He felt ashamed before his fellow villagers, so he drank by himself everyday. The runaway bride made Phuntsok lose face, too, so he asked his father again to go to Lhasa to work. His father agreed this time, as he thought his son would be embarrassed if he stayed in the village.

Phuntsok went to Lhasa that very day and found a job. Before long the family called, saying that his father had found him another wife for him and his brothers and asked him to go back for the wedding. According to Phuntsok, the runaway bride had humiliated the family. The father had become a laughing stock among villagers. One day, the drunken father went out. He returned home at dusk saying he had found another woman for his sons. The girl was quite good at weaving *pulu* (woolen fabric made in Tibet) and doing housework. The wedding was arranged for a week later.

Marriage

It was early 2003, Phuntsok's father arranged engagements for the three sons. Though he was the father, he still made some inquiries concerning the girl for the sake of his sons. A week before the wedding ceremony, Phuntsok's brother, Namgye, said he wouldn't live with his brothers. I once asked Phuntsok, "Why did Namgye say no?" He said, "Namgye said he would have no chance to find a wife in Lhasa if he got married. He wanted to live in Lhasa and set up his own family. Father said that Namgye was lazy bone but he agreed with the third son's decision. But I dared not do like him."

Since the eldest son has to take up the burden of the whole family and is the "father" of the children in the future. For other sons, they just follow the arrangement of the patriarch if they want to live together. Furthermore, they would only be regarded as "uncles" of the children. If other sons wish to set up their own families, that would be fine, but they have to bear all wedding expenses by themselves.

After the third son, Namgye, left home, Phuntsok and the second younger brother, Gonggar, were going to marry one bride together.

Gonggar was happy about the marriage. His elder and younger brothers worked in Lhasa, while other brothers were at school, and the parents were getting old, so all the heavy work was on his shoulders. After marriage, at least his workload could be shared by the wife.

The bride, Dolkar, lived in Pusong Town of Shigatse, a six hours walk from Phuntsok's family. Though the marriage was arranged early in the year, the bride and the grooms had never met. Phuntsok and his brother knew about the engagement, but they knew nothing about the name and appearance of the bride.

The wedding was celebrated in the 10 days between December 20 and 30, 2003. The date was carefully chosen by monks. It was said to be the days when Shambhala (paradise) opened its gates. Marriage during that period meant harmony for the family forever.

December 20 was the official day for the wedding. The bride was not allowed to leave early but should depart her home and arrive at the home of the bridegrooms on the same day.

According to the schedule, the people who were to pick up the bride were to leave on the afternoon of the day before the wedding, carrying things such as butter and mutton, donkeys for carrying the dowry, and a horse for the bride to ride.

As the housewife, Phuntsok's mother assigned jobs to everyone. So everything was in order. After the departure of the party going to pick up the bride, Phuntsok's family started to be very busy, frying *kasai* (a kind of deep fried dough), making wine and preparing drinking vessels of all sorts. The family hall for worshipping Buddha was cleaned and tidied with care. On the next day, it would be the place for the wedding ceremony.

Gonggar was happy and busy with the preparations for the wedding. Phuntsok hid away, reading one of Tashi's used textbooks with no facial expressions.

A square table covered with a woolen blanket was placed outside the door. In the middle of the blanket, a small square of red cloth was placed, with a symbol of *gyung-drung* (svástika or 卍 shaped emblem) made from highland barley. According to the tradition, the bride should sit on the table when she arrived. After songs and toasts for the bride, the party escorting her should sing a song in return and send a *hada* to the bridegrooms' family.

That evening, officiator Gurmey and co-officiator Ngodrup (Phuntsok's uncle) were practicing songs in the kitchen with the women who would receive the bride. In the stove, dried cow dung was burning bright to cook beef. People drank wine made from highland barley. Phuntsok's father sat in the middle, giving directions to the family during breaks.

On that evening, two more groups were dispatched to welcome the bride. The first group, headed by the husband of Phuntsok's cousin, left at 3:00 in the morning, carrying barley wine and an electric torch to welcome the bride 10 miles from home. The second group, headed by Namgye, left at 7:00 in the morning, waiting by the hill outside of the village. Phuntsok's mother and sisters were busy all night, preparing wine and other things.

At 7:30 in the morning, a messenger came, saying the group of the bride had arrived at the gateway of the village. We rushed to the gateway. In the highland barley fields outside the village, several donkeys and sheep were wandering about. The sun had just come up over the hillside, giving off a yellowish light.

As soon as I set up the camera, I heard a miserable cry. The village children told me that it was the bride crying.

Sure enough, in less than two minutes a group of people riding horses appeared over hill. The bride was crouching on the back of a horse, wearing a woolen blanket and a Tibetan hat with a flashy, square scarf. She was crying her heart out to show her unwillingness to leave her parents. The husband of Phuntsok's cousin, afraid that she might fall from the horse, was supporting her from the side.

When the people escorting the bride arrived at the gateway, villagers started to sing. The lyrics went like this: "Oh beautiful girl, you are the best jewelry. Wherever you go, you shine the brightest. Oh beautiful girl, you are like the flowers of the snow-capped mountains. Wherever you go, you are just like the snow lotus."

With the song, the bride reached the door of Phuntsok's family. People were waiting at the door to receive the bride, holding barley wine and *hadas* and *chema* (a ceremonial harvest basket).

They filled the guests' cups with barley wine and sang happy songs. Ngodrup's little daughter gave the bride a big cup of wine, but the bride kept crying. People took her finger, dipped it in the wine and made three flicks, symbolizing tributes to the Heaven, the Earth and the Buddha.

When every member of the escort party had finished their cups and taken *hadas*, they entered the door.

Phuntsok's house is the same as all houses in the agricultural and pastoral areas. It's a two-story earthen structure with the ground floor for livestock and the second floor for people. A wooden stair links the two floors.

The second floor was a square platform like a courtyard. The dowry brought by the bride was placed on a space at the right of the platform. There were three tin trunks of clothes for the bride, three handmade Tibetan quilts and six sacks of highland barley. Livestock for dowry were taken directly into the pen downstairs. In Tibet, the daughter will carry a portion of the wealth of the family as the dowry.

Lunch was prepared by officiator Gurmey and included sliced potato, Chinese cabbage and a big plate of raw beef for each table of the guests.

The bride and the bridesmaid ate in another room, not with others.

After the meal, all guests went out to the courtyard, enjoying the sun and wine or tea. At the request of Phuntsok and Gonggar, I went to chat with the bridesmaid. She told me that Dolkar had the same name as that of Phuntsok's mother. Jiayang, the bridesmaid, had married Dolkar's eldest and second eldest brothers four years ago. Dolkar, 20 years old, was her husband's youngest sister. The bride's father came as well. He told me that only one day before the wedding was his daughter told about her wedding. I asked why. The old man replied, "It's a tradition here. It's a rule made by the ancestors. It's because we are afraid that the daughter will escape and bring shame to the parents."

The wedding was to be held at two o'clock in the afternoon. There were no other guests, for according to the tradition, beside those coming to help, guests would arrive in different batches. It was set in advance which guests would come on which date.

The bride, Dolkar, had already been prepared by the bridesmaid, Jiayang, and sat on the north side by the window of the family hall for worshipping Buddha. She was still unveiled, but she was decorated with a *bazhu* (traditional headdress). Phuntsok's father said that he bought the *bazhu* from a business man from Khampa at a price of 15,000 *yuan* ($2,100 dollars). It is said to be a treasure from a noble family in Chamdo.

Phuntsok and Gonggar began changing their clothes after the bride entered the room. For a wedding, the bride and the bridegrooms must wear traditional costumes, black *pulu*, a red waistband and Tibetan boots made by

151

the family.

The hat was especially made for the wedding. Gonggar wore a headdress with a pigtail.

As usual, the seat for every newlywed was covered with a small piece of red cloth on which there was a *gyung-drung* made of highland barley. As the eldest brother, Phuntsok sat on the first seat and Gonggar, the bride, Dolkar, and the bridesmaid, Jiayang, sat next to the other. The bride's father and brothers, as well as the matchmaker, sat on the front side.

Officiators Gurmey and Ngodrup, together with Phuntsok's father, held *hadas* in their hands, standing in the center of the room. When everybody was seated, Gurmey formally opened the wedding ceremony. It began with a song by the officiators. The lyrics are: "In the backyard of my house are piles of highland barley. Don't worry about your life in the future, my dear family from afar. In the front yard of my house are butter, tea and barley wine. You can drink to your heart's content, my dear guests from afar."

The lyrics were short, but the grace notes were many, so they sang for a dozen minutes. Then the officiator, Gurmey, hung a golden *hada* on the shrine, praying for a peaceful life for the newlyweds. The second *hada* was given as an offering before the shrine along with two whole sheep, symbolizing prosperity for the newlyweds. The third *hada* was draped upon the jar of barley wine as a prayer for a happy life for the newlyweds.

With the help of Ngodrup, Gurmey gave pure white *hadas* to each of the newlyweds and extended best wishes.

During all this, the three newlyweds each betrayed their own anxiety. Phuntsok lowered his head, thinking of something. Gonggar looked around and comforted the bride from time to time. The bride, Dolkar, kept crying. She was wearing the veil during the process with her body leaning against the bridesmaid, Jiayang.

The family worship hall was full of laughter, songs and the wailing of the bride.

The women responsible for receiving guests held polished pots filled with barley wine. They sang songs of best wishes and refilled the cups of the bridegrooms. The celebration in the room reached a second crescendo with everybody cheering and singing songs. Some even danced to the beat.

The ceremony lasted about three hours, starting and ending with songs. The bride, Dolkar, supported by the bridesmaid and other people, went to the bridal chamber to rest.

The bridal chamber was on the right side of the courtyard. It has two rooms. The bigger one inside was the warehouse for highland barley, beef, and agricultural tools. The smaller one outside was about 10 square meters. At the foot of the east wall laid two plastic mats covered with new Tibetan rugs. They were seats during the day and beds at night. One of the rugs was a woolen quilt made by the family, and the other was brought from Lhasa by Phuntsok. They were folded and put together to one side. Two Tibetan tea tables were placed in front of the Tibetan rug. On the right side of the south corner of the room was placed a new Tibetan cupboard carved with patterns. Such Tibetan cupboards were supposed to come in a set of three, and the other two were placed in the courtyard. Beside the Tibetan cupboard were two tin trunks, inside which were clothes and jewelry for the bride to wear during the festivities. There was a small window through which light spilled into the room on both the east and south walls.

The bride, Dolkar, sat on the Tibetan rug. Her decorations were taken off. Her head was lowered, still veiled. Silver wine cups on the tea table were filled with wine reflecting yellowish ripples in the dark. If it had not been for the sobbing Dolkar, who was in a red veil, one could hardly have associated this small room with a bridal chamber.

Lifting the Red Veil

What does the bride look like?

Though Phuntsok and Gonggar put on a poker face and sat on the balcony quietly, they glanced secretly at the bridal chamber from time to time. According to the tradition, the bride should always wear the veil before others during the first 15 days after the wedding.

It was early for supper, so I stayed in the bridal chamber and chatted with Jiayang. At last, careful to sound casual, I remarked, "I will go back to Lhasa tomorrow. Today is the wedding day for Dolkar, but you two have not had your picture taken. How about taking one now?"

Jiayang smiled at me and looked at the others in the chamber who, just like me, stared at Dolkar, itching to remove her veil.

I read the eyes of Jiayang and drove everyone out of the chamber, closing the door behind them. Only three of us remained.

While Jiayang was taking off the veil for Dolkar, the bride turned her head away. "It doesn't matter. Only we are here!" said Jiayang lightly. The veil, with green and red checks, slid down at last. The bride, with a pair of black eyes filled with shyness and panic, gave a quick glance at me and lowered her head immediately. There were tear stains below her eyes. I didn't take the picture but sat beside her, holding her slightly rough hands, not knowing what to say.

As Phuntsok's friend, I knew that he was not willing to accept the marriage. He didn't want to repeat the days of his fathers but wanted to find someone whom he loved and who loved him. He wanted to lead a life that he had only read about in books. Many times, Phuntsok told me that, after the marriage, he will have fulfilled his responsibility. After the marriage, he would not belong to anyone else, and he would live a life of his own. But,

Men in the wedding ceremony

could I tell this to this girl who had learned only yesterday that she was going to get married? She knew nothing about her future. She was so blind and so helpless!

No matter how deeply I worried about the future of Phuntsok and Dolkar, the wedding ceremony would continue as scheduled. All guests had supper in the family worship hall. The dishes included sweet potato noodles, fried Chinese cabbage, fried sliced potato and sliced raw beef. Beside the dinner table was a small plate of salt. The swelling laughter lingered in the room.

According to tradition, after the meal all guests should drink a big cup of wine. The big cup refers to a plastic barrel that can be filled with one kilogram of liquid. Any guest who leaves before drinking up the wine will be punished by having to drink three cups more.

The drinking party seemed never to end. Women pouring wine were dressed up and in high spirits, singing songs in louder voices. As the songs rose, the spirits poured; as the spirits disappeared, the songs soared. Though the guests had brought their own cups of many different sizes, the plastic barrel in front of them was the same size for everyone. Barrels of wine were gone with the laughter, and songs and drunken faces appeared among the guests. After drinking, everybody stood and started to dance joyfully, in rows, in circles or holding hands.

The bridegrooms, however, and the bride were nowhere to be found among the merriment. Phuntsok hid in the kitchen, and Gonggar walked here and there not knowing what to do; fitful cries were heard from the bridal chamber. Dolkar was still worried about her future.

Teasing the Bride

It was midnight, yet the singing and dancing continued. According to the custom, the two officiators should ask the bridegrooms to go into the bridal chamber. According to tradition, since Phuntsok is the eldest son and the future patriarch, he should be the first one to sleep with the bride. However, Phuntsok stayed in our room and made conversation with me. His father called him several times, but he did not move. Then I forced him out.

After Phuntsok left, he hid for an hour in the toilet. His father and uncle Ngodrup encouraged him for a while at the door, and he then came out and was escorted to the bridal chamber.

There was a set of procedures for entering the bridal chamber. For instance, the clothes of the bridegrooms and the bride must be taken off and wrapped in a quilt. The officiator would then place a *hada* on the quilt and sing a song to wish them a good marriage. Also, the bridegrooms and the bride must drink from the same cup of wine. These customs are required no matter

156

how embarrassed the newlyweds; they must be observed.

This was not the end of the wedding. As I mentioned above, the wedding should last 10 days with different guests arriving each day. Presents brought by the guests would be shown and announced to everyone by the officiator at a fixed time (commonly two o'clock in the afternoon). Presents sent by one of the officiators, namely Phuntsok's uncle, Ngodrup, were first shown. He sent enough highland barley to make 40 barrels of wine, a butchered whole mutton, a pack of *tsamba*, and a pack of *kasai*; in addition, he brought gifts to each of Phuntsok's family members and every member escorting the bride shirts for the men and Tibetan aprons or headbands for the women. When he ran out of presents, they were replaced with five *yuan* for each of the remaining people.

Every presentation lasted at least an hour with the bridegrooms and bride present to sit there receiving wishes from the guests.

Phuntsok and his brother had their wedding just as their parents wished. The new family was built. But would Phuntsok's father be free of worry from then on?

In recent years, more and more young villagers from Tare were going out to work. They made money for the family and got to know new things in the outside world. Some traditional lifestyles and behavioral patterns were gradually changed. Lobsang, a distant relative of Phuntsok, was also the eldest son of his family. Since he began working in Lhasa, his parents called every week, asking him not to get a girlfriend in Lhasa. These young lads of similar ages would get together and drink since they had the same worries. They asked about the attitudes of their friends' parents and even arranged dates for one another. However, if they fell out with one another, they would expose the hidden relationship to the boy's family.

Back to Lhasa

Although Phuntsok had only graduated from junior high school, he was a fast learner. He had already mastered computer skills and Chinese while working at Kungshan. As a worker, he relied on his power to make a living. Last year he got a job at a TV station. Beginning as a janitor, he soon became a monitor, and then he was promoted to assistant producer of a program.

Phuntsok got busier, so he didn't return home often. As a result, the family grew more worried about him. He often received calls from home, and his father and second eldest sister would visit him suddenly. They even signed a contract with Phuntsok to make sure that he would not get another girl in Lhasa to form another family.

Dolkar helping Gonggar combing his hair

Half a year after the marriage, Dolkar went to Lhasa. At that time, Phuntsok was renting a house in Lalu Wetland and living with Namgye. When I visited Dolkar there, she was weaving a waistband in red wool for Phuntsok. She was still a bit shy when she met me and glanced secretly at Phuntsok from time to time. Namgye sat across the room, obviously angry with her.

In the evening, Phuntsok and Dolkar presented me with highland barley and peas from their hometown. Dolkar told me that, since the marriage, Phuntsok has never returned home. Now, as the second eldest sister is on a pilgrimage tour to Zhigongti Monastery, the parents asked her to bring Dolkar to Lhasa and to have a look at Phuntsok's life. I asked her how Gonggar treated her. She said he treated her well and so did the rest of the family. Gonggar would not let her do heavy work after she got pregnant.

When Phuntsok went out to fetch some water, I asked her which one mattered the most in her heart: Phuntsok, Gonggar, or Namgye. She said, "In my heart one of them weighs the heaviest. But I cannot tell or let others know because it is not fair for the other two." When she said this, her rough fingers touched the woven waistband. She added, "He doesn't like to go home. I don't care if he likes me or not! As for Namgye, he has been angry these days, saying I care only about Phuntsok and turn a cold shoulder to him. I haven't seen Phuntsok for half a year. Father and Mother told me to spend more time with Phuntsok, since he is the patriarch. I am caught between!"

When Dolkar lifted her head, I saw tears in her eyes. If she had not met Phuntsok but only the other two brothers, she would have given birth to a number of children and lived a long life cared for by her husbands.

Dolkar intended to spend some time with Phuntsok in Lhasa but she had to leave due to the death of her mother.

In the whole situation, Dolkar was the innocent. She was a kind and traditional girl who followed her parents' order and married into Phuntsok's family. She not only showed filial piety and respect for Phuntsok's parents but also cared about others in the family. She treated her two husbands equally. Most importantly, she was able and talented. She was good at housework, from weaving cloth to farming. The elders of the village said that few among the newlyweds were as able as she was.

The situation remained the same until this year.

Ongkor Festival

I had agreed well in advance to accept Phuntsok's father's invitation to spend the Ongkor Festival in the village. When I was about to go, Phuntsok said he was too busy to go himself. So he asked Namgye to accompany us. The roads to the village had been widened. The pathway to the mountain was deserted. Instead, a wider road that could allow a tractor to pass had been built along the river and the mountain.

When we arrived, Phuntsok's father and Gurmey were sewing. Gonggar told us that these clothes were prepared for Ongkor Festival, which was approaching rapidly. Seeing Namgye's return, Phuntsok's mother felt happy. She poured the barley wine for him. Namgye showed his father his newly-obtained driver's license. Everybody had a look and was happy about it. Gonggar showed no interest in the driver's license. He sat on the Tibetan rug and focused on sewing clothes. In Tare Village, needlework, such as making clothes, shoes and embroidery, is done by men. Women don't know how to do it.

After a while, Phuntsok's eldest sister, Gezong, came in. Seeing me, Gezong was very happy and gave me a big hug and a large piece of cheese she had brought along. Gezong looked better than she used to

Namgye and Dolkar

160

years ago. Her husbands have separated, and Gezong lives with the eldest. Now her husband doesn't beat her any more. Her two daughters are being brought up by her family. With the financial support of her family, she also had her new house renovated this year.

During the year, some families built new houses. The village committee set up a satellite receiver for TV and radio signals. In addition, four families installed telephones. Phuntsok's family was one of them. In Tare Village, people have lived a dull life apart from their own entertainment. What interested them the most were the new possessions that other families bought. New "properties" in a family meant a polish on the face of a patriarch, and families who have installed telephones seem to be enjoying a higher social status in the village.

When I saw Dolkar again, she was not as shy anymore. I could tell that she had become a member of the family. Phuntsok's mother used to get up the earliest; now it was Dolkar. There was a cowshed under the rooms where we lived. Before six every morning, there was the sound of the gate being unlocked, and we would hear Dolkar taking the cows to the corridor where she would milk them. By the time the whole family got up, Dolkar had finished milking and making the butter tea.

During these two days, Dolkar always entered my room at dusk, giving me water or a cheese. She would sit a while, as if she had something to say to me, but each time I asked her, she would change the subject.

In the night, Phuntsok's mother came to my room. She closed the door carefully, and held my hands after some hesitation. "I want you to help me do something, but you should keep it secret from Dolkar!" I could tell she meant it, so I agreed.

"Tell Phuntsok, if he insists on getting married in Lhasa, we will not disagree now. But he must get a good girl and a good job. He should live a decent life. He should not find someone indecent."

161

Dolkar cutting weeds

Phuntsok's mother's words surprised me. Just yesterday, she had said she hoped Phuntsok would come home. "Auntie, what makes you change your mind?"

The old lady said: "I think you are right. We hoped Phuntsok would stay home for his own good. But Phuntsok doesn't like such a life. If we insist, he will not be happy all his life. He won't come home for the Ongkor Festival because he may worry that we will not allow him to leave."

"Does uncle think so too?"

"We have discussed it and he agreed. But for the time being we cannot let Dolkar know, for when they married Phuntsok was the patriarch. If Phuntsok won't come back, he won't be the patriarch and the family of Dolkar won't agree. We are not going to tell her until she gives birth to the child. And Tashi has agreed to stay home and live with Gonggar and Dolkar. Two sons at home are enough." Tashi was Phuntsok's sixth brother, who was 16 this year and a student of grade three of junior high school. Phuntsok's mother was calm when she said this, as if she had already thought it through.

With the changed minds of his parents, could Phuntsok be free from his worries?

On the second afternoon, Dolkar was going to cut weeds to feed the cows. She asked me to come with her. Namgye and Gyatso went along. When they got to the destination, Dolkar told them to leave us alone and took me to another place far from the brothers. A big rock lay there, so that Namgye and Gyatso couldn't see us. Dolkar and I sat on the ground.

"Why doesn't Phuntsok come back? Is he really busy at work?" Dolkar asked, lowering her head and trembling.

Though I knew what she would ask, I still couldn't answer that question. I saw with my own eyes how Dolkar came to this family and how she accepted her life. I couldn't deceive such a pure-hearted woman.

"He hasn't come back for a long time, but I dare not telephone him. Villagers from Lhasa said he didn't want to stay home. Last year, when my brother sold butter in Lhasa, he heard that Phuntsok had a woman in Lhasa. He even came here to argue with Phuntsok's parents." Dolkar stopped, as her tears started rolling down her cheeks.

"You are a member of this family already. And they love you. Gonggar is very kind to you. Phuntsok has adapted himself to the life in Lhasa. He has a good job. He may never be able to come back to work on the farmland," I said.

"My aunt just told me one day before the wedding that I would get married in Tare Village. Phuntsok is the patriarch of the family. I cried and hit my father with a shoe, but I still came the next day. Now Phuntsok is so ruthless. What on earth does he want?" Dolkar shed her tears and cried even harder.

"I am hurt by Phuntsok. I am true to him, really I am…" Dolkar leant against me. Her tears couldn't be stopped.

During that afternoon, Dolkar told me a lot about her and the three brothers of Phuntsok. I understood that, among the three men, she cared the most for Phuntsok. I knew that Namgye liked Dolkar, but he seldom came home. So I thought that the two of them should stay there together for a while.

In the dusk Namgye, carrying a huge bundle of weeds, returned with the empty-handed Dolkar. They talked and laughed when they were walking in the sunset.

His parents convinced, Phuntsok was at last relieved, but he worried that his name was on the marriage certificate. If Dolkar refused to divorce, Phuntsok couldn't feel at ease at all. Fortunately time will change everything, he said, since the toughest problem has been overcome. He believes that Dolkar will one day understand him. He is looking forward to that day!

The Youngest Woman PLA Soldier Entering Tibet

By Li Jiajun

In 1950, the No. 18 army corps of the People's Liberation Army (PLA) soldiers marched into Tibet with the aim to turn a new page in the history of the snowy plateau. Among the 40,000 troops entering Tibet were 1,100 women including more than 70 Tibetan women from neighboring Sichuan and Qinghai provinces. Together with the male soldiers, they climbed snow mountains, stood guard, herded yak, lived in tents, and sang and danced together with the rest of the troops.

These Tibetan women soldiers could speak both Chinese and Tibetan. This helped connect with local people and publicize the Party's policies. Three of them were only 11 years old. Their names will be marked in history forever: Gao Shizhen (Kelsang Droma), Little Tsering, and He Ping. Why did they want to leave their parents and join the army? How did they overcome the hardships when climbing the mountains to Lhasa? How did they manage to grow up? What was it like to witness the peaceful liberation, democratic reform and socialist modern construction that changed the lives of so many serfs on the plateau?

In 2005 Gao Shizhen retired from the position of vice-chairman of Standing Committee of the People's Political Consultative Conference of Tibet Autonomous Region. She returned to Sichuan and settled down in Chengdu. Her black long braid has become gray, but she tells her story in the same characteristically straight-forward manner that she used all her life.

"I Have No Regret."

It was incredible that an 11-year-old girl would want to join the army. "To be honest, I knew nothing at that time of what it would involve. I just felt I would be very proud to be a woman soldier."

Gao's home was in Derge County, in Xikang Province at that time. In late 1949, when the PLA marched towards southwest China, Liu Wenhui, the then warlord and governor of the province, surrendered. In the spring of 1950, many PLA soldiers rushed to this ancient small town beside the Jinsha River. The town was full of merry melodies of songs about liberation. Gao deeply felt the sunlight of this new life.

She was told that the PLA soldiers would move westward soon towards the south Silk Road to liberate Tibet. Everyone was preparing yak and forage to support the frontline battles. Her brother was among the first to join the army. Gao envied him very much.

In October, a group of women soldiers came to Derge. Most of them were Tibetan girls from Ganzibiz and Kangding. They wore two small braids and green uniforms, walking proudly on the ancient stone steles roads.

An idea came to her mind suddenly that she could be a woman soldier too! At that very moment, Gao made up her mind to join the army and go to Tibet.

The commander looked carefully at the girl. He thought that she was just a child, and so weak. How could she get to Lhasa, which is a thousand-mile-

long harsh journey across mountains and rivers? So he refused at first.

Gao cried and argued that why some other women soldiers at her age could join the army. Some women soldiers came around and pleaded her case, saying she was from a poor family and a good girl.

Still feeling reluctant, the commander agreed to discuss the issue with the local department concerned. The next day, Gao went to the office of the county government. Local officials were touched by her determination so they broke the rules and recruited her.

However, she was too small for the uniform, so her sister soldiers had to fold her trousers and stitch them up. But Gao did not care. "It doesn't matter. I will grow taller and fit into them some day."

Before the army headed for Chamdo, the commanders took her to say goodbye to her family. Her two younger brothers were very happy. But her father was unhappy because he thought she was too young to be a soldier. She was not as tall as the musket. He knew the hardship of tramping over hill and dale. His heart wrenched and grew a bit angry, hoping that she could leave home when she grew bigger.

The next day, the father insisted on seeing his daughter off. He walked along with the army and talked to her and they made peace. In this way, Gao Shizhen left her hometown and her family, setting her foot on the expedition to the border.

The first stop to Tibet was Chamdo. The brief battle of Chamdo was just over when they arrived. The local government of Tibet sent a delegation to Beijing to negotiate peace.

A cadres' school was set up in Yunnanba, Chamdo. Gao was in the first training session for Tibetan soldiers to improve her knowledge and learn about the Party's ethnic and religious policies. The girl realizing she had a responsibility together with her brothers and sisters to drive away the British imperialist threat, support the unification of China and construct a new Tibet.

All of a sudden, Gao understood her mission and decided to dedicate her life to Tibet.

A Busy Young Interpreter

After the Agreement of the Central People's Government and the Local Government of Tibet on Measures for the Peaceful Liberation of Tibet (also called "17-Article Agreement") was signed, Gao was assigned to be an actress on the performing arts team and headed for Lhasa. She was short, so she was always cast as a child in the performances.

She was so young that her fellow soldiers helped her carry bags. On the road she and an actor named Qamba would sing songs for the soldiers in return. Though they were a little immature, soldiers were moved by the passion of the performers.

No. 18 Army Corps was also responsible for publicizing and connecting to the local people. The performing arts team's role was broadened so that they could be of service wherever they were needed.

When they passed through a valley on the west of Lhorong, there was in urgent need of an interpreter at the newly-established Xobando Military Depot. The commander found that the little actress was good at Tibetan and Chinese. The depot decided to invite her as an interpreter for two months.

Xobando is the inevitable entry from Xikang to Tibet. The military depot was newly established, just with a few shabby log cabins and military tents, yet burdened with all the transfer missions of materials and pack-animals for all soldiers of the No. 18 Army Corps.

It lacked a lot of things. For matters as big as buying forage and hiring livestock or as small as borrowing needles they would need help from the local government and people.

Interpreter, as a matter of fact, grew into "liaison officer" between

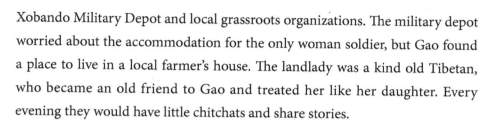

Xobando Military Depot and local grassroots organizations. The military depot worried about the accommodation for the only woman soldier, but Gao found a place to live in a local farmer's house. The landlady was a kind old Tibetan, who became an old friend to Gao and treated her like her daughter. Every evening they would have little chitchats and share stories.

At that time, people had little trust in PLA, and strange rumors were spread by the upper classes of the Tibetan nobility. As a graduate of the cadres' school, Gao could cut through such rumors and provide explanations.

Thus, she not only provided rich information about local society to the military depot, but also publicized the Party's policies on religion, as well as PLA's tenet of serving the people, and its rules and regulations. Gao suggested that the performing arts team members get together with neighboring villagers. She also visited grassroots tribe leaders and poor people together with the head of the military depot.

The relationship between the army and the people grew closer. For some time, villagers didn't know the name of the head of the military depot, but they all knew the woman soldier.

Every time commanders of the army made a stop at Xobando, they praised the work done in the military depot. The commander of the depot would refer to Gao's efforts. "Little Gao has done a great deal for us." Before long, commanders Yin Fatang and Zhou Jiading of the No. 52 Division heard reports from the commander of the depot. They asked her to go with them to Lhasa. She had been longing for Lhasa for a long time. It was her ultimate goal. So she agreed immediately.

On the day when she left Xobando Military Depot, villagers brought eggs, cheese and big pancakes to see Gao off. Gao kept in mind the PLA's rules about such offerings and gently refused to take the presents.

Her landlady insisted on giving her the big pancake she just made. "You are my daughter. How could a daughter refuse pancakes made by her mother?"

Gao was moved into tears. She felt reluctant and then broke the pancake into halves. She gave one half to the landlady and kept the other half. It was deep affection for the landlady that she took.

At that time, the Xikang-Tibet Highway was not open to traffic. One had to travel across a number of rivers, such as the Jinsha, Lancang, and Nujiang as well as 17 mountains above the snow line, such as Dayamal, Yigongla, Dendara, Wahe, Lengla, and Sera mountains.

Soldiers met many troubles, such as the cold, lack of oxygen, the weight of their backpacks and attacks from bandits. It was not an easy journey for the 11-year-old Gao. Looking back upon the past, she was most touched by the warmth of her revolutionary family and the care for young Tibetan women soldiers.

Gao Shizhen had to make more efforts than ordinary soldiers. Her feet had many bloody blisters. Every time when she fell behind, some soldier would offer help.

It was winter when they climbed Lengla Mountain, which was a world of snow and ice, with howling cold winds blowing. Gao was exhausted and often dizzy.

As the army went westward, the logistics became a headache. Though it was clearly stipulated in the "17-Article Agreement" that "local government of Tibet should help PLA purchase and transport provisions and other daily necessities," the Tibetan authorities refused to implement the agreement. The PLA was confronted with a shortage of food.

Gao remembered after they climbed Sejila Mountain, there was only rationed yolk wax for food.

"It was new experience for us at the beginning, but after eating this day after day, we got bored of it and felt hungry. The leaders gave out a dozen of fruit candies to the soldiers. Many elder brothers gave their candies to us, 'Kids love candies, but we adults do not,' they said. Little Tsering and I believed that

was true and took all the candies. When we grew up, we understand that both adults and kids love candies. They just shared the candies so that we would not be hungry.

"When the army arrived in Medro Gongkar, two days' walk to Lhasa, the unit held a meeting. The head told little Tsering and me, 'You need not to participate in today's meeting. Go and have some fun.' Little Tsering and I sat outside the tent chatting but we couldn't help listening to the meeting.

The truth was that there was only enough *tsamba*, Tibetan barley cakes, for two more days. They agreed to leave the *tsamba* to little Tsering and me so that we would make it to Lhasa."

Gao couldn't help crying when she recalls this. "How sweet the soldiers were and how sweet the army is! Many of the new recruits suffered from such a hard environment and now had to double their effort!"

Dancing into Gyantse County

After many hardships, Gao arrived in Lhasa but her division moved on to Gyantse County. She had no time to visit the famous Norbulingka (Summer Palace) and Barkhor Street, but had to set out for Gyantse County and return to the performing arts team after half a year's absence.

Gyantse County connects to Lhasa on the east and Shigatse on the west. On the south is Yatung, an important military town lying on the border with India. It is a place of special military importance, as it connects to dBus, gTsang and India.

In 1904, a most severe battle between Tibetan people and British invaders took place here, earning it the name of "City of Heroes." The young Gao was moved by such patriotism and loved the land. She stayed in Gyantse County, and became an actress, a member of the democratic reform team, the head of the performing arts team and, secretary of the district committee, and finally deputy secretary of the county committee. She lived 20 years there.

The No. 52 Division stationed in Gyantse County, taking charge of protecting the territory and helping local people with production. The performing arts team's rehearsals and performances of singing and dancing, drama and short play were centered on the core ideas of the "17-Article Agreement."

To publicize the Party's policy and establish closer relation between the army and the people, many performances in towns and villages were organized. The team walked dozens of miles carrying the heavy gear. When they got to a destination, the performers would immediately make up and start the performance.

Gao's performance was part of a group dance that combined Xinjiang, Tibetan *Sgor-Gzhas* and Xianzi dances in Batang, to show the unification of the ethnic groups. Because she was small she still played children's parts in the drama and short plays. The audiences loved her.

When they were not rehearsing or performing, they were needed to build camps and plough farmlands. At that time, Gao was only 12. She had little strength. So she was sent to help with cooking and delivery of food and water. She would also help wash bed sheets and clean house for her elder sister soldiers. The division awarded her for her efforts and even the performing arts team began to perform dramas about her deeds in touring performances.

She grew up into a woman in these circumstances. She never regretted when she looked back. From Derge to Gyantse County, she changed from an ignorant little girl to a person that knows well how to be of use to people.

In June 1957, Tibet Working Committee streamlined organizations to carry forward the Central Committee's policy. Gao was transferred to the working committee of Gyantse County youth league, and was assigned a task to accompany a number of youth from Gyantse County to the Tibet Youth League School to study in Xianyang.

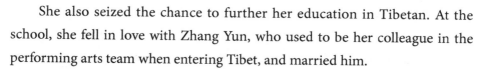

She also seized the chance to further her education in Tibetan. At the school, she fell in love with Zhang Yun, who used to be her colleague in the performing arts team when entering Tibet, and married him.

In the spring of 1959, the PLA soldiers stationed in Tibet put down the rebellion and started the democratic reform. The young couple was excited about the news. They applied to return to Gyantse County. The husband could not leave immediately because of his work at the school. But Gao couldn't wait any longer. She quit the study in advance and went back to Gyantse County alone.

Gao Shizhen joined the work team of the democratic reform. She did a lot of work in the towns of Zakui and Dongpu in upper stream of the Nyang Qu River. She mobilized, redistributed land and livestock, and established grassroots organizations. After the celebration, she was assigned as the vice head of the publicity team of Gyantse County. She was ordered to rebuild the Gyantse County performing arts team.

Gao, under instructions of the branch working committee to make full use of local talent, recruited some Tibetan students. She personally went to Yatung, Nakartse and Panam counties to select actors and actresses. Thirty-five young people, all of whom were children of liberated serfs, were chosen. These Tibetan children spoke little Chinese and were not well educated but Gao had confidence in them. It was how she had grown up after all.

"Tibetan people have a gift for singing and dancing. Those children were better than I when I started. Gao invited a music teacher and a dance coach to help. They all lived in a shabby house at the foot of Tsong Mountain, and kept practicing every day. This is how the performing arts team was rebuilt.

"It was the way in which I grew" was the way that Gao Shizhen asked her students to proceed. She was strict with the students. Those girls, in particular, young, slim and good-looking, had attracted many young lads. To ensure their safety, Gao did not allow them to go out much. She believed that it was a golden time for them. They should spend the days learning and practicing, rather than talking about love.

After half a year, Gao shifted to performances. Whenever the music teacher and the dance coach had a good idea or she received good scripts, she would immediately start rehearsal. The first performance, centering on the Party's work and containing rich ethnic features, created a sensation in Gyantse County. After that the team gave road shows and performances across the county. In a time when cultural life was scarce, she delivered precious spiritual comfort to people.

There were no vehicles at all. They had to travel by carriage or on foot. Cold bread was their food and the ground for threshing barley was their stage. This had been Gao Shizhen's experience, and she imbued them with her spirit. At the same time she passed on the invaluable traditional teacher-student relationship of Old Tibet to the next generation.

In spring of 1963, Gyantse County created a performance called "The Song of Harvest," which won a top prize in the region. Then Gyantse County was merged into Shigatse, and the majority of the team was enrolled into the Tibet Singing and Dancing Troupe. They also became the backbone of a small art troupe on horseback. All of these young men and women are still good friends of Gao.

Three Provincial Senior Officials from Niandui District

Gao's home became silent as her students went off into new areas. Leaders asked if she would like to transfer to Shigatse. She thought about it for a long time. She spent more than two decades in Gyantse County, which had become her second home town. How could she be willing to leave?

In November 1963, the branch working committee assigned her to become deputy secretary of Niandui District Committee of Gyantse County. At that time, Gao's son was a toddler. When her husband Zhang Yun worried

174

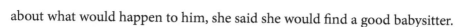

about what would happen to him, she said she would find a good babysitter.

Niandui District is situated at the upper stream of the Nyang Qu River. Gao was very familiar with the place and she felt quite at home. Soon, though, she realized the difficulty of working at grassroots levels. The former secretary of the district committee was transferred, so was another deputy district chief. When Gao took up office, she was alone.

She had no one to turn to when she needed help. The current publicity campaign about the need to "investigate and research" instead of just follow orders and the importance of "seeking truth from facts" in the newspapers gave her inspiration.

After making sure that her child was under good care, she visited grassroots officials and others and listened to them. For two months, she went into the villages of the five towns. She gained an all-round knowledge about the harvest, water facilities, the life of the people and security.

It was her first time to develop work in the countryside. She was not sure how to create a harmonious environment for the 4,000 liberated serfs and build the socialist new countryside. She came up with several plans, but she could turn to no one for help. She felt stranded.

Gao requested many times to be assigned a secretary of the district committee and a chief for Niandui. "I promise I will give full support to them." Wu Yunlong, deputy secretary and head of department of organization, told her that the county committee was at the moment short of staff.

So she had to find talent from grassroots officials. The heads and Party secretaries of the five towns of Niandui District were all liberated serfs. Though they were not well educated, they had done well in putting down the rebellion, carrying on the democratic reform, reinforcing water facilities, and leading people to the way of prosperity. They had high understandings of politics, close connections with local people, and rich experience in work at grassroots levels. Why not try to find capable people among them?

Some leaders like to create "yes man" for their second in command so that they will carry out orders. Gao, however, was a good listener for the truth. She conducted examinations and selected a dozen of grassroots officials in five towns and then submitted a list of three to the prefecture committee.

Sandrol from Dongpu Town was the same age of her. He joined the Party after the democratic reform. A smart man, he was once a teacher, vice head of the agricultural association, and head of town and secretary of the Party branch. He was spoken highly of his work by the head of the county committee.

Gonjo, branch secretary of Liaoyuan Town, was from a good family. He was an elder and enjoyed a good reputation.

The youngest was Phuntsok, who was just 20 years old and secretary of the town's youth league. He was vice head of the county's people's work team. He was brave and a role model in the support to the battle front in 1962.

The organization department of the county committee was glad to see the arrangement. However, Tibetans at that time were not yet part of the official government of the country. The procedures for hiring and promoting such officials were very complicated and time-consuming.

Gao was impatient. She visited the county's departments often and checked the progress of these applications. Finally, in the first half of 1964 the appointment letters arrived. At last, the district committee meeting of Niandui could be held.

Gao was promoted to be the Party secretary. She asked everybody in the district committee meeting to always speak the truth and respect and trust each other. All of them would implement the plans and measures that were passed together.

Niandui District took the lead in production and improvement of people's lives. More and more farmers built houses. Niandui was awarded many times by the county committee and the prefectural Party committee.

In 1965, Gyantse County sent Phuntsok to further education at the Tibet

College for Nationalities. It was a busy time for Niandui District. Gao was a bit unwilling to send one of her best. However, she agreed after thinking twice, since it would be a chance of a lifetime for Phuntsok. The decision laid a solid foundation for Phuntsok who went on to be secretary of Gyantse County and Commissioner of Shigatse in the future.

In 1966, the 10-year Cultural Revolution brought disaster to the countryside of Tibet. The continuous fighting in the rest of the region disturbed people's lives and production. In Niandui District, however, people figured out how to carry on production. The 4,000 people were well fed, their lives were good, and the society was stable. It was a miracle.

Gao was transferred to Lhasa in 1973. She served as deputy director of Women's Federation of Tibet Autonomous Region, deputy secretary of the CPC Lhasa Committee, and director of the city's people's congress. She made great contributions in putting down the riot in Lhasa and maintaining social development and stability. In 1998, she and Phuntsok were elected vice-chairmen of People's Political Consultative Conference of Tibet Autonomous Region. Sandrol was promoted in 1995 to standing member of the Party Committee of Tibet Autonomous Region and secretary of Party Committee of Shigatse. In 1998, he was head of the United Front Work Department of the Party Committee of Tibet Autonomous Region, and vice-chairman of political consultative conference of Tibet Autonomous Region.

The old friends from Niandui gather from time to time. People say it was wonderful that Niandui turned out three great provincial leaders. Sandrol and Phuntsok still remember the help they received from Gao, and at the same time Gao Shizhen is quite grateful to her former colleagues as well. They helped her do the work she loved which was to build the Tibet of the future.

Democratic Reform Diary at Kesong Manor, Lhoka

By Lin Tian

June 6, 1959

I went to Kesong Manor together with the trial operation work group for democratic reform. The work group for trial operation of democratic reform would work here for a few days.

Setting out in the morning, we went through Nedong Village, going southwards along the Xiangbu River. From the foot of one hill to that of the next, the broad valley plain was a sea of green wheat, grass and flowers. A stream bubbled and flowed through the field. There were willow forests and monasteries with red eaves and golden roofs everywhere. At the river mouth were water mills. Birds twittered under the azure sky. Tibetan countrywomen worked and sang in the field…What a picture! In the past, such pastoral settings were set against the miserable lives of serfs and slaves. Until now, when they began to think about their own liberation.

As the sun rose higher, we got to a place with multiple water channels and abundant crops. From a distance we saw a house as big as a fortress with purple eaves. From one corner was the beginning of a thick forest.

This is Kesong Manor. Rumor has that it was the place where old Surkang, ancestor of the head of the rebellion group Surkang Wangqen Geleg, started his golden days.

When our vehicle got to the village, naked children came over and said hello. As soon as the car stopped, the villagers came to help us carry luggage and brought us into the manor.

It was an ancient stone-made square-shaped three-story building, a typical residential manor. Around the courtyard was the stable and warehouse. A few steps away from the entrance was a large stairway, on which were marks made by bare feet. The halls in the middle of second and third floors were the living rooms and scripture hall of the serf-owner, separated with large black curtains. On the two sides, opposite of the living room, were other rooms and

Serfs threshing at Kesong Manor before the liberation

the kitchen. We were to be on the third floor. The big empty house smelled of dust. There were quarreling sparrows and swallows under the exterior eaves. The entire house gave off a sense of eeriness.

On the second floor in the kitchen, an elderly woman took care of the cooking stove. She had fluffy and disorderly grey hair, with a dull look in her eyes. We heard that, she had been a *nangzan* (slave) in the manor since she was a teenager, now she was more than 50 years old.

Besides *nangzan* and *chaiyao* (a kind of slave for farm work), nobleman had serfs. These were divided into *tralpa* and *duiqoin*, a kind of serf who plowed a small piece of land, paid a poll tax to the master and did certain corvee labor.

Mangers circled around the big house on the first floor which could accommodate hundreds of horses. But all the horses had been taken by the rebellious serf-owner. By the door to the manor was a manger as big as a canoe.

An old groom lay under the manger. He had been a *nangzan* and had kept horses for 40 years. In all his life, he lived in the stable in winter and on the roof in summer. Sometimes he used to lie under the manger. Upon arrival of the work group, he was given a room.

That afternoon, the work group convened a meeting for all manor serfs to elect members of the Preparatory Committee for the Peasant Association.

The bright sunlight penetrated into the grassland which was supposed to be the venue for the meeting. The bubbling stream flowed along the edge of the forest. The bells on the necks of the donkeys rang all the time as they ate grass in the bushes.

All the men and women, adults and children in the manor, came out from the surrounding small huts, or from the stables on the first level, or barns in the exterior courtyard. They sat on the grass. Just by glancing at the crowd, one could understand what serfdom meant.

Few of these 200 people, old or young, wore a full set of clothes, only rags with patches or greasy stains. Women and children were all bare foot.

A white-haired, half-blind elderly woman, Ngodrup Tsomo, became a *nangzan* when she was eight years old and kicked out when she was 60. She had been begging for three years. Her three generations from her mother to her children were *nangzans* as well. Qimei Tsomo was her mother. Her face was like a withered orange. The daughter was black and thin, with messy hair, holding a skinny child.

You will not believe her child was 10 years of age. Since he was malnourished he was only as high as his mother's knee. He was already registered as a *nangzan*.

Only the lads and girls with dirty feet were lively. They smiled and talked about something.

Now these people would become their own masters for the first time.

The meeting started. People lifted their heads, with their mouths half open, listening to words that they had never heard before.

Comrade Zhang of the work group said: "Fellow villagers! Today we, who have suffered tremendous pain and been groaning under a yoke for a long time, hold our first meeting. For what?

"We know that your master Surkang participated in the rebellion and has ran away, and the manager of the manor fled too. Those who stepped on you have been brought down. We will elect our own people to lead us, to liberate us and help start a new life for ourselves.

"Who will lead us? Will we illiterates be OK? Will women be OK? All will be fine, as long as he or she is kind, fair and trustable."

The audience chuckled.

"We will set up an organization for peasants, namely a peasant association. Today we will first set up a Preparatory Committee for the Peasant Association."

Selecting the candidates of a Preparatory Committee for the Peasant Association

For the past two days, people had been thinking, compared and selected the candidates and today the list of candidates was published.

"Our Chairman is Nyima Tsering!"

People looked at a young man in the crowd. He was brown-faced, with a pointy forehead. His eyes were deep, but a bit naive. This short young man substituted for his dead father and became a *chaiyao* (slave for farm work) in Kesong Manor 15 years ago when he was nine.

When people heard his name, they mumbled, "He was a poor child. He would not lead us the wrong way!"

"Vice chairman is Jijia!"

People's eyes searched for the tall girl with a broad face. She was shy, kept her head lowered, with her hands touching her ragged skirt. She was a *nangzan* too.

When it came to life experience, she said: "I didn't grow up by having *tsamba*, but by painful experience!"

Her master fed her with three quarters of what a worker needs, but made her do the work of two and a half people. Of course people had faith in her.

Another vice-chairman was Wujin, a *tralpa* with a yellow face. Other members of the association included Ngawang, Dorje and others. The total number of members, including chairman and vice-chairman, amounted to nine, of which four were *nangzans* and *chaiyaos*, three *duiqoins* and two

tralpas.

The crowd was divided into three groups for discussion. Among the group of *duiqoin*, an old man with burns and wrinkles stood up. With half an eye, he was still stalwart despite his poor life.

His name is Lhazhu and he said: "Fellow villagers! For the first time we have become our own masters. We can select our own people to lead us, not to oppress, hit or scold us.

"Nyima Tsering is young, Jijia is a woman, but they are our own people. I watched them suffer pain since they were toddlers. They won't lead us the wrong way. They won't abandon us.

"We should turn over a new leaf. We should be free. We should have good days now, if we elect people like them. We just woke up from a deep sleep. We need people selected by the Communist Party of China and ourselves to lead us forward…"

The crowd smiled, but no one spoke. They had been slaves for so long that they were not used to voicing their own opinions.

After a long time of silence and giggling, an old woman whispered: "What the official said today was from the bottom of his heart. I will pray for whoever we elect but I don't know how to express myself. I don't know what to say!"

Then she clapped her hands and said with trembling body: "Thank you so much!"

The group of *tralpa* was very active. Though they belonged to the landlord as did the *nangzans*, who had absolutely no freedom, they were more knowledgeable so they had much to discuss about each of the candidates.

At last, people circled round the grass under the sunshine. Nyima Tsering, Jijia, Wujing, Dorje and Ngawang stood in front of a table in the middle of the circle. They were sweating but their eyes were bright with joy. People surrounding them held their hands high.

These hands used to do the work of others. Today, for the first time, they put them up freely before the manor. For the first time, they enjoyed the fruit of the democratic reform.

Chairman Nyima Tsering spoke, "Every fellow villager!"

When he spoke, children started to giggle in the audience. They couldn't understand what the *nangzan*, who used to sleep under the master's roof and dared not raise his head before the master, was going to do. The adults stopped their childishness.

Nyima Tsering continued: "Fellow villagers, Chairman Mao and the Communist Party of China liberated us! Since you have chosen me, I will do my job well. I hope all of us will unite and eliminate all bandits, rebels and wrong doers. Only then can we move on with our good lives!" The audience gave him warm applauses.

After the election, there were words like:

"He is so talented. Nyima Tsering is so talented!"

"We need leaders like Jijia, indeed, otherwise who cares about women *nangzans*!"

People said that when Wujin, the kind and a bit woozy poor *tralpa*, came across something happy, he would not tell his mother or wife and instead take a pot of wine made from highland barley and looked for his friends to celebrate. But this time, he is now one of the leaders. Several pals would be coming and celebrating with him.

In the evening, the newly-elected chairman and members of the committee met. They had *tsamba* paste for supper and went to the manor. They came up to the third roof. But the four female members of the committee hesitated when they got to the door of the old scripture hall of Surkang.

They said, "Let's meet in the stables downstairs instead!" or "Why not change the place to grass area of the Linka?"

The gloomy big room gave them horrible feelings. According to the old rules, women, specifically female slaves, were not allowed to enter the scripture

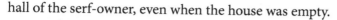

hall of the serf-owner, even when the house was empty.

Comrade Chen of the work group said: "Come in! It's your own home. What are you afraid of! Let's hold the meeting here." They entered the room quietly.

Eight members of the committee (one was absent) and some staff, held the first meeting of the Preparatory Committee for the Peasant Association. They first discussed ways to deal with the chief and the local tyrant. These were the henchman of Surkang and the manager of the manor.

For years these two were loyal servants of Surkang. They spared no mercy to serfs. And when people didn't do it quickly enough, they would lash and kick them. During the several months when the rebels were here, the chief made everyone go out to forage and he beat people frequently.

At the start the two *tralpa* members of the committee revealed many crimes of these two.

Wujin said: "These two guys did so many bad things. Now everybody knows that they have been arrested. Their fates are up to us!" But he wouldn't make such a decision about their punishment by himself.

Nyima and Jijia had their own idea which was to hold a mass meeting, bring them in front of everyone, and then punish them with labor. They reached a consensus with this idea.

The work group asked Wujin: "Do you really agree?"

He answered: "Sure! It is not just above the neck (it's not just words), but below the neck (it's heartfelt feelings)!"

When everybody walked out of the main assembly hall, it was getting cool. How nice was the wind in the early summer!

June 7, 1959

At noon, I met the old woman Qimei Tsomo outside the gate by the pool. That evening we visited with her.

The old woman had white filthy hair and wrinkles and wore a rough brown shirt made of ox hair and wool. This was her only clothing, which also served as a quilt at night. She was black with dirt, thick-skinned and quivered when she spoke.

She could not remember so many things. She only remembered that her mother was a *nangzan* of Surkang Kesong Manor for quite a long time and her father was a *nangzan* of a big *tralpa* and served as corvee labor for the *tralpa* all year round. One winter with a heavy snow, her father was sent to Nakartse to run errands but never came back. People heard that he died there.

Before long, her mother was blind. The steward would give her some food when he remembered. Soon, her mother starved to death. At that time, Qimei Tsomo was only eight years old.

The woman used her hand to illustrate: She put her hand three inches above the ground, meaning that she had been very short. Although there were many empty rooms in the manor, *nangzans* never have been allowed to live in them. They were only permitted to sleep in stables, barns or the corridors under the eaves.

As early as she could remember things, she lived in a shabby shack for frying highland barley or lived in the stable. First she took care of the children of the manager of the manor and then began to brew highland barley wine, weave, pasture cattle, and cut grass as she grew older.

Every morning, the steward gave her a little *tsamba*, a cup of tea, and very little butter. She had to work hard all day and then was given a bowl of *tsamba* paste at night. In winter, snowy winds blew into the shack. She crouched under her ragged clothes, freezing and hungry. In summer, rains blew into the stable and she'd be soaked in rainwater mixed with horse manure. When pasturing, she was not allowed to return early. If she returned earlier due to rain, she would be beaten and scolded by the steward. The woman never married. She bore two children with a man who

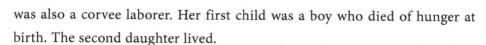

was also a corvee laborer. Her first child was a boy who died of hunger at birth. The second daughter lived.

At the age of 40, she cut off a finger while scything grass. Blood kept trickling down from her hand and she fainted.

Her 15-year-old daughter Zhuma cried: "Mom's finger was cut off!"

She cried and reported to the steward, but nobody took care of her mother. They didn't have any medication or bondage to bind her up. The wound got worse. A *nangzan* came up with an idea. He took some butter, boiled it and put the wound into the boiled oil. She fainted with the pain once again, but her finger got better.

The steward did not care whether she was alive or dead and sent her to pasture cows the next day. She had never lived in a decent room, nor wore shoes or socks. She always felt hungry. She had never been fully dressed nor had her own home. This is typically the life of a *nangzan*!

June 8, 1959

The rainy season came soon to Lhoka. We had a shower today.

In the morning, we listened to briefings of the work group. At Kesong Manor, if the estate-holder saw that certain *tralpa* had a little good farmland and few laborers, he would force the transfer of one or two persons to that *tralpa* and make them *nangzan* and serve corvee for the landlord.

By doing this, the landlord made some people of the *tralpa* families into slaves. Twenty out of the 44 *nangzans* of Kesong Manor were such people. Sometimes the master of a *tralpa* family died, and the family would not be able to plow the land. The estate-holder would recollect the land and use *nangzan* to plow.

Moreover, many serfs and slaves were husband and wife, but they didn't have a family. For example, *duiqoin* Zeren Dorje and a girl of a *tralpa* family were a couple. However, if Zeren lived in his wife's home, he would be a *nangzan*, while the *tralpa* wouldn't allow his wife to live in Zeren's home. So they had to live separately. Only at night, Zeren slept at his wife's. In addition, if the husband and wife were both *nangzans*, but with different families, they were not allowed to live together and form a family.

This was serfdom. It also showed that the load of corvee for the serfs was heavy and that serf-owners took advantage of the system to appropriate laborers and peremptorily cause abnormal relations between serf couples.

That night, at the gate of the manor, I met Kelsang, the groom of the manger of the manor. Being a short, bitter-faced man, he always wore a shabby hat. He was an interesting *nangzan*.

His parents were poor *tralpas* of Yalongka (a manor of Surkang, several miles away). From nine years old, he was sent to Kesong Manor to pasture cattle and groom horses. We asked why he was so short.

He said: "I have been oppressed from my childhood!"

Even when he was over 30, he was still a heavy corvee labor.

After his parents died, he couldn't plow his own farmland, so the manager of the manor recollected the land and the livestock, and assigned them to another family. Then he himself was given to the family as a *nangzan* in addition to his long-time corvee for the manager.

His new master gave him one *sheng* (1/20 of one *ke*, about half a kilo) of *tsamba*, and another *sheng* every five days. We asked him how much one *sheng* was. He said, "Two bowls." We asked how big the bowl was.

He said, "Neither big nor small."

We asked how big exactly the bowl was. He couldn't describe it but grabbed a wooden bowl from the corner of the stable. We asked if that would be enough for him. He said, "Only two bowls. That's OK for a morning." "What about the nights?" He laughed and patted his belly, meaning empty stomach. Everyone smiled bitterly.

The poor man lived a life of half hunger. He was over 50 years old, but had never worn boots or shoes. Every year the manager of the manor would give every person serving long-term heavy corvee labor two *ke* (a *ke* of highland barley is about 14 kg) of highland barley from income of the land. Kelsang exchanged these highland barleys for some clothes. In autumn, he would pick up some highland barley when he pastured horses and he traded those for some salt and tea.

He didn't live in a house though he worked for the manor for 40 years. He lived on the roof of the stable, even when it snowed. Only on rainy days would he get down and hide in a corner of the stable. He never tasted meat unless at the Tibetan New Year the serf-owner gave him porridge with some meat slices. He was beaten often. He said the steward had a big nose and an ugly face. The manager of the manor was a white faced fox, who was "educated" but ferocious. He imitated the big nose steward and the white face of the manager, disgruntled and spitted: "Du! Kelsang, where did you go?"

The two beat him so much that he even lost count of those beating:

"Much more than my age."

"Sometimes I was not there when they called me. When I arrived, they grasped my hair and beat me with anything that came to their hands, such as a horsewhip and a stone! A couple of times, my ass and waist were beaten blue. These two are not humans, if the PLA soldiers catch them now, I shall take my revenge."

He said that whenever they went out he needed to prepare the horses and wait for them to mount. He also needed to remember the direction they went so that he could wait for them to come back. If he was not there waiting when they came back, they would beat him with the horsewhip.

We asked him whether he saw the big noble Surkang. He said he saw him once. He came by car once about two or three years ago. A few days before he came, the manager and the steward asked *nangzans* and heavy corvee labors to clean the house, polish windows, and put up new scripture banners on the door.

When he arrived, we stood in the doorway to welcome him, taking off our hats, lowering the head and sticking out the tongue (expressing awe). When Surkang was leaving, he gave each labor 5 *liang* of Tibetan silver (15 *liang* of silver equal one silver dollar of the time). He had been a slave in Surkang's family for 40 years, with the 5 *liang* Tibetan silver being the only reward.

Kelsang would go everywhere with his ragged hat.

He explained: "Though it is worn, it cost me 60 *liang* of Tibetan silver! It was nice when I bought it. I have had it for three years."

It was his only property.

"Where did you get the 60 *liang* of silver?" I asked.

"I accumulated it bit by bit!"

It was dark and starting to rain. Kelsang was cold and shivering. We asked about his wishes.

He thought for a second and said, "I heard that they will raise the salary for *nangzans* and heavy corvee labors. Two liter of *tsamba* for everyday. When will that begin?"

This Kesong Manor was not the manor where the old Surkang family began. That manor was at the southern foot of the mountain. During the time of the 5th Dalai Lama (300 years ago), one of the family became a "Senben Kampo" (one of three major attendants of Dalai, in charge of a Dalai Lama's daily life).

Old Surkang forcibly took over this fertile land and built a new manor. It was said that one could look at the three Holy Mountains when he stood on the roof, so it was named "Kesong Manor" (Manor of the Three Fortunes).

In this manor, there were over 1,200 *ke* of lands (*ke*, or *dou*, a *ke* of highland barley is about 14 kg. One *ke* of land meant a piece of land that could accommodate one *ke* of seeds, about one *mu* or 1/15 hectare). He had over 300

serfs (including adults and children). It was said that Surkang owned a dozen manors and pastures. This was only one of them. Surkang family lived in Lhasa and he had a manager.

June 9, 1959

I went to Kaimo Manor in the morning. It was about 1.5 kilometers away south from Kesong Manor along the Xiangbu River. By the road were stone-built dykes and bubbling water. Along the banks were willows and a kind of pointy shrub. Wild roses were blooming in the woods and thrushes were singing.

Kaimo Manor was the manor of Kaimo, who was a great noble in Lhasa. It was a big house with purple eaves, with forests and pools all around. In front of the gate was a scripture wall made of stones, on which six-syllable mantra prayers were carved.

Entering the gate, there was a big black poodle hanging about the entrance. In front of the second gate there was a chained black dog. At the end of the second gate was a wide stairway similar to that of Kesong Manor. Judging from the big poplars around the manor and the stairs, the manor must have a history of two to three centuries.

The manager of the manor had been arrested for his participation in rebellion. No more than 20 *nangzans* lived in this large house. People from the work group also lived here. We went to the second floor, and saw that women doctors from the work group were giving medical treatment to serfs.

The leader of the work group introduced the situation of the manor to us, saying that its scale system and ways of exploitation were much like those in Kesong Manor.

In the manor, there were 34 serf families, including 16 *tralpas* and 18 *duiqoins*, in addition to 21 *nangzans*. There were also a dozen of *chaiyaos*, who were laborers transferred by the manager from *tralpa* and *duiqoin*. The leader of the work group said that the *nangzans* were eager to be emancipated.

Returning back to Kesong Manor in the afternoon, a meeting was held there by the Preparatory Committee for the Peasant Association. Wujin, Nyima Tsering, Ngawang and Jijia came and waited at the corridor. Nyima Tsering was very happy and said: "I am full today. I have had four bowls of *tsamba*!"

June 10, 1959

At Kesong Manor, a general meeting was held today to scold and denounce the rebels and local tyrants. From the morning, the manor was full of people, including members of Preparatory Committee for Peasant Association, barefoot women, men wearing shabby hats, and even old serfs. At noon, men, women, old and young gathered around in the shade of the Linka in front of the manor.

The meeting started. The steward, who had been a chief of the rebels and Surkang's agent in Kesong Manor, ran away. Now, the chief and a local tyrant who followed the steward in many bad things were taken to the venue. Nyima Tsering, the lad who had been a corvee labor from age eight and was now the newly elected director of Preparatory Committee for Peasant Association, for the first time wore a pair of boots and had his face washed.

He stood in front of a table, saying: "Dear fellow villagers! Now the meeting begins. In the past, the noble Surkang, stewards, and chief exploited us for so many years. They rebelled, hoping to stop the liberation. Now, the Central Government and PLA soldiers helped us combat them, drive them out and destroy them. Now we stand on the grounds of the manor! We are holding such a meeting against such inhuman treatment for the first time..."

Then he listed the crimes that the chief and local tyrant had committed. He said: "Our pain was like a river flowing through countless years. Today, we

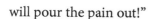

will pour the pain out!"

After Nyima Tsering finished, Wujin came up and said: "Today we are denouncing these two. In the past, we had to keep our mouths shut, now the exploiting classes have vanished. Serfs now are free.

"The chief and local tyrant followed the steward's orders to beat us. They helped the bandit rebels rob us. When the bandit rebels ran away, they helped them hide ammunition and carry valuables and foods from the warehouse in the manor to their own homes. These are ours!"

An old woman stood up and exposed: "They also hid a number of guns, ganged up with reactionaries and await their return."

A young man named Baigan stood up with a gasp and said brokenly: "I was beat by them so hard that I could not speak. My sister and I picked up barley from his land, then he beat my sister and I."

A girl with wild hair stood up and cried. She was a 13-year-old orphan, named Pema Yuzhen. Her father was a poor *tralpa*. When she was little, her father died while doing corvee. Her mother carried her on her back and plowed the lands. Once the mother quarreled with a henchman of the lord, and the local tyrant beat her half dead. The mother crawled home, bleeding, and died the next day with the child in her arms. Pema cried.

An old woman with hair as white as snow, eyes staring blankly, wept with tears running down her cheeks. She opened her arms and cried out: "Please help us, the Communist Party of China, the People's Government, every fellow villager please supports us..."

All the audience were crying. The elder woman was Pema's grandma. She spoke out about the common experience of serfs. The sounds of grief and indignation sounded like thunders in spring:

"Overthrow the evil serfdom!"

"Eliminate exploitation and oppression!"

It was agreed before the meeting that there would be no violence at the meeting and attendants were not allowed to bring iron or clubs. However, Wujin suddenly walked forward as he was listening, and took out a short club and hit the back of the local tyrant. This tall local tyrant fell over, and bled from nose and face. And this made some angry people start to show sympathy for local tyrant. A little *nangzan* of his, who wore rags and was hit by the serf-owner many times, now cried for mercy for the serf-owner.

Nyima Tsering dragged Wujin to the other side so that the denunciation of the lord and their agents could go on. The rage went on and on.

June 30, 1959

This afternoon we visited Kesong Manor again where all *nangzans* have been liberated. All 51 families have established homes except those old or weak and the disabled. Walking into the manor, the deathly atmosphere was long gone. Instead, there was vital life force everywhere. Kids were singing around the fences, while a carpenter was making a small blackboard. The primary school was about to open.

A liberated serf getting her own cow

In the manor 10 families of *nangzan* have settled down. After dinner we went to their houses which were clean and

194

spacious. They were having *tsamba*. Every family was newly-provided with daily utensils, a bag of *tsamba*, a bag of highland barley, a small dinner table, sickles, pickaxes and so on.

We were moved when we visited home of Dorje. When Dorje was 10, her parents died and the land was taken back. Thence, the sisters and brothers all lost their freedom and became *nangzans*. They had been separated since then. Now they were liberated *and* reunited and all moved in together.

They were very happy. The older sister Dorje said, "Today little sister stayed home to pasture the donkey and goat and make tea. My younger brother and I went out as casual laborers. After the harvest and land division, we will have our own land. And we can afford to buy some clothes."

July 1, 1959

We visited Nyima Tsering and his family. His old mother was very happy. There were two little calves chained at the entrance and an old goat at the door. His mother was making butter. Now she had two cows, one of her own and the other was distributed by Nyima.

We talked to an old woman about the liberation of *nangzan*.

The woman said, "We had suffered great pain from very early times. I had only my son Nyima Tsering, whose father died when he was very young. I had tough days to raise him to age eight and then the steward made him a *nangzan*. I gave birth to my son, but he belonged to others and he couldn't come back freely!"

She spoke to her son, "Oh, my son! Since our ancestors we have been poor but good people. You are a good child. You don't steal and you don't do anything bad. Now people elected you chairman of the Peasant Association, you must do good things for the poor people!"

When she was speaking, a tall old man with beard came in. He was

Nyima's stepfather, a furrow master. He went to work early and came back for lunch. Putting down his spade, he took out some grass for the old sheep, then sat down, opened wide his sweating clothes.

The old woman gave him a big spoon of wine made from highland barley. He drank several bowls and ate *tsamba*, stewed radish and mutton with her.

When it came to the allocation of lands, the old man said all people here loved to work. If the lands were given to them, there would not be a weed on the land. They were waiting for it. They were already thinking: what piece of land would I get?

Jijia moved into her new house three days before we visited her. She sat on the ground covered with a blanket, and was giving tea to a neighbor with a big smile. It was Nyima Tsering. He was late for lunch so he came to her home to have *tsamba*. At a corner of the room was her deep basket full of highland barley, a small basket, an old box, and cooking utensils on the stove. We asked about her thoughts after liberation, but she refused to talk about it then.

At night, Xiao Drolma of the work group came and Jijia began to talk when she saw her. She was cooking *tsamba* paste as she talked about the past with us:

"We were born to suffer tribulation. We eat what they don't eat, wear what they hate to wear and step on the paths they don't want to go. We couldn't even think about having a family. We were not free. Although I am a member of the committee, I am still young and know little. I will learn from others and do my job well. After the autumn and we divide the lands, I will pay back the debt of 2 *ke* of highland barley and plow the land well."

July 23, 1959

The liberated serfs were working on the rain channels and red flags could be seen flying everywhere. The site was bustling.

We went to the home of Dorje, now chairman of the Peasant Association, who was leading the construction. His 31-year-old wife was at home, which was extremely poor. Beside some jars and rags, there was nothing. Dorje was a *tralpa* as was his wife. They had a small piece of land. The couple settled down living on the farmland and did some casual labor. They had two children.

At noon, some men and women left the progress for some tea. They brought *tsamba* and a little tea, salt, oil, alkali, etc. Everyone brought something. Dorje's wife made tea.

In the afternoon, he told us he was thinking about the resettlement of the more than 100 liberated *nangzans*. Among them were two servants of the manager and they wanted to return home immediately. He asked them how they could live if they went back home with empty hands. He wanted them to stay until after the distribution. The poor had no *tsamba* to eat and he had food for only a few days.

We asked what he was going to do. He said he would borrow. From whom? From these families who had more land. He meant the rich *tralpa* families.

We asked him how he would borrow. He said that in the past he had to give the rich *tralpa* families eggs and meat before he could borrow food from them. Then they asked for high rates return. Now the new government has ruled that there will be no rates for borrowing food. We have to lend these to him.

His words made us laugh. He also said, now the people were happy and the Peasant Association had power!

July 29, 1959—July 30, 1959

In the afternoon, we went to Kesong Manor. It rained several times and then we finally had sunny days. The highland barley came up. The original barley seed is tiny, but now it has produced a green sea. The rape flower withered and now was podded. The pea flower bloomed, like little butterflies, some were podded too.

Kesong Manor village was very tranquil. The women were pulling grass and children went to school. Inside the manor, members of the Peasant Association were having a meeting. They were making the final plan to divide the land, which was about to be announced soon.

They were busy checking farmlands. There was over 1,600 *ke* of land in the manor in various sizes.

One representative from each family had a meeting in the forest. Danba Gyansen of the work group sat in the middle holding a list. People crowded into the place and heard the results. Then they were divided into three groups for discussion.

During the discussion, *duiqoins* and *nangzans* said, "When we were born we were doing things, but we never had a piece of land. The new government, like parents, has treated us equally and given lands to us all. Yesterday, the meeting suggested reducing lands from the mid-class peasant. At that time we asked for their opinions and they agreed. Today, when we announced that the lands of middle-class peasant would not be touched, they felt happy."

They said that they now had no disagreement about it. A middle-class peasant Sonam got drunk when he heard that his lands might be taken, saying: "You got your lands (referring to *duiqoins* and *nangzans*), but I had a huge lost."

Today, he was relieved. Yesterday, some *nangzans* didn't want to have more lands fearing that they would have to run corvee. After the officials explained, they were relieved.

On the night of June 29, a meeting was summoned by the Peasant Association. They studied how to divide the land, then they decided to divide the land in Caddo Village. The 30th of June was the first day of land division and I came to witness the historic moment.

The next morning, a huge crowd poured into Caddo Village. We walked along with them. Xiao Drolma took along a board, like a painter. It was for writing in the field. On the road, old Lhazhu spoke to Nawang Dingzeng,

"The people's government treated us well and even is more considerate than those who have a daughter to marry to a man. It has treated us equally."

In the past, poor parents could only leave debts to their children, while the people's government gave people farmland. They were talking and laughing. They went over a river quickly and didn't care about the water.

When we got to Caddo Village, the members of the Peasant Association began the meeting. An old man suggested, according to the situation, if they were given 8 *ke* of land, then it should be 5 *ke* of good land and 3 *ke* of bad land. Everybody agreed, so the division started.

Who would be the first one? A dozen families who should be given land took a rock, knife, a key or something as their own mark, and handed it to Ngawang, a member of the association. Each one was represented by a number.

The drawing started with Siwei Badrup. He is an old and short furrow master. The second one was Tsering Tsomo. First she was given a fallow land of 2 *ke*, with lavish grasses. She carried her baby and went there happily, asking Wujin to tell her where the boundary was. The third one was the elder woman called Sonam Qunzong, who was given fallow land as well. Her lips parted in a delighted smile, immediately moved to the haystacks and stone piles to make the marks. The elderly woman lived with a child. They got 7 *ke* of land.

Little Drolma took the board, recorded one after another. Then he convened a meeting for those who had been given lands.

In the evening, the Peasant Association held another meeting to study the work for tomorrow. Jijia reported that Tsering Tsomo was very happy. She asked for opinions. Yixi Zhima and Zanjan (two *duiqoins*) said that they had never owned lands. Now they had lands, thanks to the thoughtful efforts by the

Harvesting on the land that belongs to her

Communist Party of China and the new government.

Nyima Tsering reported, Chaguo (a widow with two children) was extremely happy tonight. She said, "I used to take children to do casual work, or carry them to beg. Today, the government gave us food and land, and now we don't have to worry about food. With the land, I shall work well. Life will get better. "

Jijia quietly added, "We have lands, but no people wearing pants (meaning no husband)."

Everybody was laughing. Jijia flushed. She was also thinking about someone to wear the pants! Liberated serfs were full of joy today. They had beautiful wishes!

For much of the past century, especially since the reform and opening-up policies were adopted some 30 years ago, the Tibetan economy developed, and the face of urban and rural areas really changed. People of the snowy land were becoming rich.

I am a Tibetan. I have lived and worked in Lhasa for decades. I have witnessed these changes with my own eyes. I showed my records and share them with those friends who care about Tibet and would like to know more about it!

Witnessing the Tibetan Democratic Reform

By Suoqiong

I

"I was completely dedicated to work relying only upon my proficiency in Tibetan language."

Lhazom Dolkar, in her 70s, is a vice-chairwoman of the Lhasa People's Political Consultative Conference. People often see her in the media and on various occasions because she has such great power and energy.

Born into a peasant's family, I was never a noble but my husband Gomperlha, on the other hand, was an officer in the local government. At that time the local government needed to find some young men from Nimu and Ai to form the retinue of the Dalai Lama and help the Dalai as scribes. Generally the retinue from Ai was called Aidrup, and those from Nimu were called Nidrup. They were looking for children from decent families, with good looks and smart minds.

My husband Gomperlha was Nidrup. At that time, he was the only boy at home. A son needs to carry on the family, so his father asked the official of Nimu County to seek a marriage alliance instead but he failed. So my husband went to Norbulingka. He learned to write as he worked.

He made huge progress in his studies while attending the Dalai Lama who favored some of the kids and called them "Jiansai" (meaning specially favored). The term bears another meaning – "Yanmu" - because the 13th Dalai Lama appointed his men to be private investigators to learn about people's lives in order to improve the society. My husband was one of them.

My husband was perhaps the most famous one of the Jiansai. He also served the Dalai Lama wholeheartedly. As a result, people from all walks of life spoke highly of him. He was sent by the Dalai Lama to personally handle issues with the Kasha (the former local government of Tibet). Although he wasn't from a noble family, he was respected by many nobles. (This was before I met him but I heard about it a lot.)

In 1933, when the 13th Dalai Lama died, some nobles spread rumors that Gomperlha had not taken good care of the Dalai Lama and had given him wrong prescriptions. He and several others were found guilty and sentenced to execution, but instead he was exiled to Kongpo. He stayed there for several years and then went to India, where he worked as an assistant to the business manager of the Reting Monastery.

Sometimes he stayed with Amdo Gedun Chopel. The two learned that the British were going to invade Tibet. The Tibetan people in India were against such an invasion. After much discussion they set up an organization and sent Gedun Chopel to the border as a spy. But the Indian police learned of the matter.

The Indian police department wouldn't allow Gomperlha to live in Delhi, so he had to move to the countryside. He couldn't go back to Tibet. So he contacted the Chinese Embassy in Delhi for assistance to go to Nanjing.

When he got to Nanjing, the conditions were harsh. The office of the

Dalai Lama wouldn't offer help because he was considered a traitor by the local government. He found a job with the help of the Commission for Mongolian and Tibetan Affairs and earned a monthly stipend. Because of sharp devaluation of the currency in central China, his money became almost worthless. I heard that he ate a bowl of noodles a day and lived on the meager pay of the Commission for Mongolian and Tibetan Affairs.

The Nanjing government fell and some parts of our country were liberated. He applied to return to Tibet in 1949. He took a roundabout route to Tibet, passing through India.

He had nothing left in Lhasa by that time. He rented a house on Yutuo Road. After the peaceful liberation of Tibet in 1951, the local government of Tibet arranged accommodation for the staff of the Preparatory Committee for the Establishment of Tibet Autonomous Region, and he moved to Dacai. Later he reported to the new local government that he was back but was living on nothing. He asked them for help. The local government allowed him to live in the new palace in South Barkhor Street, the residence of Tupden Gomper before he was exiled.

My ancestral home is Rinpung. I went to Lhasa for a prayer ceremony in 1954. Gomperlha and I knew each other, because my third sister had married into his family in Nimu County. After Gomperlha resumed his office in the local government, I married him. My mother went with me to his home, which was huge.

We had just met. I wanted to go home, but he wouldn't allow me. I still went back and lived at home for a few days. After I came back to Lhasa, Gomperlha wanted me to go to the public school for adults that had been recently set up.

At first, I refused. For one thing, Tibetan women had never gone to school or participated in government work before. For another, my mind was bound by old habits and traditions that only children need to go to school.

But he said that I was young. If we were to catch up with the revolutionary route of the CPC, we had to learn a lot. He well understood the difference between capitalism and socialism, He said that I would find it hard to get a job if I received no education. So I went to school. At school, I found a mother of three children was there too, so I accepted it more easily.

I started to learn Tibetan and literature, Chinese, arithmetic, politics, as well as the content of the 17-Article Agreement (the Agreement of the Central People's Government and the Local Government of Tibet on Measures for the Peaceful Liberation of Tibet). The school also offered lessons on ethnic and regional policies.

At first, I was not good at Tibetan, but with study, my Tibetan improved. Afterwards, just like he said, men and women became equal. He also said, "In addition to equality of men and women, equality of ethnic groups will also be achieved, and then you will have the opportunity to work." His mind had been broadened and his vision sharpened due to his journeys to India and central China. Thanks to his far sightedness, I got the chance to learn.

After the peaceful liberation of Tibet in 1950, the PLA really improved people's quality of life. In particular when Gyantse was flooded, the support for the disaster-stricken areas was very powerfully apparent in terms of food and all other necessities. Such support wouldn't have been seen in the old society. The PLA granted loans to the people, established schools and publicized the Party's policy and education. Every time a meeting was held to unite the frontline, they accorded us a rich reception with candies.

At that time, the army was faced with difficulty. Though the country was powerful, there were no transport facilities and transportation was very difficult. However, they would never leave people working on the front lines empty-handed. The army helped the people with farm work and provided them with free medical care. In prayer ceremonies they gave a lot of silver dollars to the lamas. The CPC members were not believers, but the policies of nationality and religion they carried out suited the actual situation of Tibet. So the people deepened their understanding of socialism which laid a solid foundation for democratic reform. Still, during this period, I heard that some people of the upper class reported to the Central People's Government that the people were not satisfied, so the reform was delayed. Nonetheless, all young people who wanted to go to study in central China were sent there.

The Tibetan people, at that time, were looking forward to democratic reform. But the Central People's Government didn't rush it since the upper class of Tibet was reluctant. At that time, I was asked to study in central China. But my children were young, my mother was more than 80 years old, and I had just gotten married so I didn't go. Instead, I poured my energy into working for young people in Tibet, and I never stopped.

I came to Lhasa in 1954. In 1951 Tibet was peacefully liberated. The PLA soldiers entered Tibet. They strictly followed the regulations (the Three Main Rules of Discipline and the Eight Points for Attention). Life in the army was tough. We peeped through the small holes in the walls and saw that they were cooking peas. They never borrowed from the people. For example, they would immediately pay silver dollars for firewood. They did many good things for the Tibetans and showed great respect for us. They brought benefits to the local government and people, including help in production and support in agriculture.

The income of civil servants in local government doubled from 1954 to 1959 including salaries given by the government and earnings from the people. Those nobles lived a more comfortable life than before. Many goods were imported from India. Banks were established and granted many loans to Tibetan businessmen. I know this because I knew some business people who imported goods of all sorts. Nobles led a comfortable life and the people had gained unprecedented help. As a result, the society made general progress in all fields.

The request for reform was postponed and finally a rebellion took place. It was obvious that the rebels had very little strength. They claimed to have support from the USA, that support didn't have any foundation. So, the rebellion in Lhasa in 1959 was put down the next day. The nobility, headed by the Dalai Lama, fled to India. Still some nobles stayed on the right side with the party and the people.

After the democratic reform, the Tibetan people gained real freedom and their human rights. The people became their own masters and overthrew the three major estate-holders. They lived a happy life and production capability increased. The property of those who had joined the rebellion had their estates confiscated including houses, lands and livestock. Those land owners who had not been in the rebellion could take advantage of a policy that allowed them to get compensation. The confiscated materials and lands were given to the people.

A movement against exploitation of serfs and slaves by the serf-owner class, including three major estate-holders—former local government, aristocrats and upper-ranking lamas in the monasteries was launched. In the past, the three major estate-holders, who only made up 5 percent of the population of Tibet, owned all cultivated land, mountains, waters, serfs and slaves, while the ordinary people, accounting for 95 percent of the population, had nothing to rely on for their living. From the year of democratic reform, laborers were the beneficiaries, instead of estate-holders. Since then farmers and herdsmen have lived happy lives. When the autonomous region was founded in 1965, local officials who hadn't joined the rebellion were assigned to various positions. No matter what critics may say, we have lived a good life. My children have jobs and I have a sufficient life. The CPC's policy was to help people become prosperous. The people gained power and political, economic, cultural and other fields have been developed.

In 1977 the Lhasa People's Political Consultative Conference was established. I was elected a conference member, and I have been working in that office ever since. At that time, we reinforced political study, provided for the production of vegetables, and helped the municipal committee and cultural administration prepare materials for exhibition halls under the Potala Palace. In 1982 I was elected a standing committee member of the conference. In 1984 the Chengguan District and Doilungdeqen County People's Political Consultative Conference was set up under Lhasa. I was appointed vice-chairwoman. On October 10, 1984, I was elected the first vice-chairwoman of the district's conference. For about 13 years I worked in Chengguan District and was busy with anti-secession campaigns. Though I cannot read Chinese, I was completely dedicated to work relying only upon my proficiency in Tibetan.

In 1997 I was elected vice-chairwoman of Lhasa People's Political Consultative Conference. Besides, I have been a member of the Tibet People's Political Consultative Conference since the first session. The year before last, I wanted to retire because I was getting old, with poor memory, hearing and eyesight. I had an operation in Beijing last year and I got better so they wouldn't let me retire. Except for meetings, I don't have office hours. My family is fine; I have a daughter and two sons. They all have jobs.

II

"We sisters became the first female tractor drivers in Tibet."

When Kelsang Yudron retired from Bayi Farm in 1988, she was only 48 years old. Now the old lady lives a good life. She has sold a resettlement home built years ago and moved into a new apartment. There are two cute dogs living with her.

My hometown is Pengbo. When I was little, my parents gave me to our relatives. They didn't have any children, so I became their child. Their home became my home. I lived with two elderly people whose home was on a piece of cultivated land. Usually I did farm work. Sometimes I did work for a manor in the village reaping crops or threshing wheat. I did what they told me to do. During breaks, I did household chores.

In later years my relatives died, so I returned to Lhasa. My mother didn't have any cultivated land, so I went to the neighbors' fields in the fall to glean dropped highland barley and worked for others to earn some money. It was my life.

I have two siblings, but they didn't have jobs. They only wandered about. When the PLA soldiers entered Tibet, we ran to see them. In return, they said hello and gave us food I had never seen before. Villagers said the PLA would give us poison so we should not accept what they gave. They also said the PLA soldiers would cut off our ears for food, so children were scared. But all these sayings turned out to be rumors. They kept us from getting closer to the PLA soldiers.

Later the PLA soldiers started to recruit workers so I joined. We went to Bayi Farm to work as manure collectors. There were several of us at that time, but now they have all passed away. Our superior wanted me to go to the Central University for Nationalities in Beijing, but I didn't go as I didn't speak Chinese and I was a bit intimidated. Later the boss sent me there to learn to drive a tractor so that I wouldn't waste my best years in life.

Along with the PLA soldiers, we cultivated wasteland and planted vegetables. Some of my Han colleagues asked about my feelings about being a female tractor driver. I told them I was happy, since I was single, young and healthy. I wanted to work every day, and had no sense of fear. I worked around the clock.

I observed the rebellion of 1959 which was stamped out in a couple of days. We were very pleased to be liberated and wouldn't have to live a life of poverty and hunger. At that time, I was young and easygoing, so I didn't feel tired at work. The army came to work as well. Sometimes there were many of them. I felt happier to work with them.

Because I was young, people usually let me take the easier jobs. I worked hard. I felt really happy. Then some of my colleagues got jealous and made complaints to the boss.

In 1959 when the rebellion was about to take place, I was at Norbulingka collecting manure. At that time, Tibetan troops were stationed in Norbulingka, too. When we passed by, these soldiers scolded us and threw stones at us. We dared not respond a word and left quietly.

During the rebellion, we dug many burrows in Bayi Farm and hid there, using tree branches and military uniforms to cover the entrances. When gunshots sounded in the night, a Han woman brought us together immediately and asked us not to scatter. She arranged us in the burrow of Qiyi Farm and gave us food. The rebellion was promptly put down. I saw that the Tibetan troops tied a *hada* on a stick and went in the direction of our farm. At first I didn't even know what that meant, but later I knew it was surrender. There were some injured Khampas by the river, who were borne on stretchers.

At the beginning there

Becoming a female tractor driver in Bayi Farm after the democratic reform

209

was no carriage in Bayi Farm. We used camels to carry manure at first. Then we had four carriages and four trucks. Then I learn to drive a tractor. We used it to carry everything except grass. I sowed seed and felt happy to see the green cultivated land.

Now poor people have more ways to work and to have a better life. I feel very proud to have driven such mechanized equipment and cultivated land in Tibet! I met the man there who later became my children's father. After I had a baby, I could not do this kind of work any more, so I was sent to the vegetable group. This was my life.

I have four children. I retired in 1988, when my husband was physically sound and my children had jobs. Now my oldest daughter has been retired for two years. She has a daughter who just went to college this year. Under the leadership of the CPC, people can live a happy life. That's what I think.

III

"Why did I organize mutual-aid teams for the poor?"

Tsering Lhamo likes her photo album very much. She brings it out whenever someone visits her. At her house in Tsedang, the old lady showed us her favorite photo album and pointed to a new picture in it: her participation in the art troupe of senior citizens, during her visit to Beijing for the Olympic Games. (She spoke highly of the hospitality of the people of the capital.) She was smiling in the picture, looking quiet and calm like a younger person. The old lady said: "Laborers are the healthiest," especially people like her, perhaps, who has spent her entire life in labor on the farm land.

I was born in a serf's family in Sangarcholin, Lhuntse County. I had been a servant of estate-holders since I was six years old. The children of the estate-holders were well fed while I was feeble and weak. Sometimes I washed diapers, sometimes I fed them and sometimes I carried them on my back. They were too heavy for me to carry and fell down. Then the estate-holder would slap my face. I was badly treated and suffered from shortages of food and clothing.

From age six to eight. I fetched firewood in the mountains. If I fetched enough, I would have a bowl of "Tuba" (similar to dumplings); if I fetched less, I would have no food and be badly beaten. At the age of 12 I was sold to another manor by the estate-holder. Those heartless estate-holders cared not at all about the feeling of serfs. Wherever we went, we could not escape from the social system. Serfs could only suffer misfortune but never experience happiness. After I got to my new master, I had not the slightest break from pasturing or working. I worked until I was 32.

What we can take away with us is only the shadow behind us, what we can leave behind is only the footprint on the ground.

In the old society, I had a child when I was 25. We had nothing to feed him at that time so the wretched baby died of hunger. I never forgot that pain. The PLA soldiers, shedding their blood and sacrificing their lives, freed us all. From the day of liberation, the sun rose in our hearts. I heard that when my mother was giving birth to me, she tore a piece of rag and covered my body with it, telling me not to steal, not to lie and to work hard. After the PLA soldiers came, they gave us a house, a cow and sheep. They granted me the rights of a human being and various means of production for a living.

I took the lead in establishing a mutual-aid team. At that time there were six groups in four villages. Then the order came from superiors to divide the big groups into small teams—mutual-aid teams. The six big groups were divided into 20 small teams. At that time, those experienced families with the means of production would have tea and wine together. Some of them founded their own mutual-aid teams.

Another 11 families used to pasture sheep, horses and mules for their manors or do some household chores. They were not lazy guys, but they were not skillful in production because they did not know how to plough. As a result, nobody wanted them. So I decided to set up a mutual-aid team just for them so that all earnings would be theirs if they sweated for it. I reported the idea to our district leader and he agreed. So the 11 poor families established a mutual-aid team.

Although we were confronted with a lot of difficulties, we still overcame all problems with the help of government leaders. At that time, the estate-holders and nobles didn't believe that we could organize our own production. They thought that we would give up and become serfs again. Some people even asked, "How can they plough if they can not even cook?"

We didn't lower our heads; instead we spent more time than others on work. Without livestock, we carried manure by ourselves. In the harvest season, it turned out that we had harvested the most among all 21 teams and we were awarded by the county and prefecture. We felt more confident. We

Tsering Lhamo (first left) with all her members of the first mutual-aid team established by liberated serfs in Tibet

often discussed production, so our production developed more and more. Our lives got better day by day. We donated all excess grain to the country.

We felt that, though we were poor, we could still achieve greatness as long as we had spines. The most important thing was that the feudal serfdom system had been abolished, and we had gained personal freedom. We all understood that by following the CPC could we find a way out.

In 1965, the People's Communes were set up. We donated the largest sum of money and materials, including horses, cows, sheep, food, and so on. These were not only my own contributions but efforts of all the team members.

The children of this "team of the poor" received a good education and the children of seven serfs became civil servants. We owed a lot to the Party. In addition, with the help of the state and some provinces and cities, our county developed more successfully than other places. We could not imagine then how good our life could be. People have built buildings like manors. All the furniture inside is new. Now we can live completely by our own hands.

IV

"President Jiang Zemin encouraged me."

After the peaceful liberation of Tibet and particularly since the 1980s, Nyima Udrup, with his diligent and down-to-earth nature, immediately benefited. His was the first big farming household, and he was named a national model worker. In 1990, President Jiang Zemin met with Nyima Udrup in Shigatse. He encouraged Nyima Udrup to plow more lands. A serf who dared not look at the "master" of the manor now had the feeling that he was a master of the country.

The place used to be called Ganbo Manor. Gangdrup Chamqiu, the master of the manor, was the head of the local government. Born in Longxa of Tongmenda, he lived in Lhasa throughout the entire year. He would bring five servants and a housekeeper and come for five days in autumn's harvest season. When he was not here, the manor was taken care of by Nieba who managed a servant, a foreman, a donkey keeper and a production manager.

We were *tralpas*. I have liked work since my childhood, but we couldn't feed ourselves well since the majority of the harvest was taken by the estate-holder. At that time, there were five members in my family. We worked in a tiny farm community and lived in several dark houses. There were only about 20 families in the whole of Ganbo Manor, all working for the master of the manor. I remember that at that time the master of the manor would change every three years between the noble family and the monastery. Simply put, Gangdrup Chamqiu would rule three years and then the upper-ranking lama of Drepung Monastery would rule the next three years (the harvest of the manor was shared equally by these two estate-holders). Every time the master of the manor changed, the *tralpa* families would collect 10 eggs from each piece of land for the master, hoping that he would treat us well. When the master, especially Gangdrup Chamqiu, was inspecting the manor, everyone was afraid of him and no one would dare look at him.

My family rented 15 *mu* (1 hectare) of Gangdrup Chamqiu's land and provided laborers to work for him. If a laborer failed to go to work, the estate-holder would come to the family and threaten us. They had strict management over the farmland. If the *tralpa*'s livestock ate grass on the land of the estate-holders, they would lock up the livestock, and the owner of the livestock would be called and blamed. If the livestock owner dared return a word, he would be slapped or even lashed. Moreover, there were corvees of all kinds sending foods to Nieba when he was inspecting the farmlands and going on errands to Lhasa or Shigatse. After every harvest, Gangdrup Chamqiu would organize over 20 donkeys to transport the new grain to Lhasa or Shigatse. What about the rest of the grain? He would ask the *tralpa* to organize livestock by ourselves to carry his grain to a huge granary in Gagang, Shigatse for free. How were we supposed to live? Some gathered and discussed filing a lawsuit in Lhasa, but they wouldn't have won as they had no training.

Like others, we worked hard, but every year we were in debt. Some villagers starved to death; some died during famine, and the population became smaller and smaller.

After the democratic reform in Tibet, our life got better. All gains were ours so we became more active. A few decades later we bought three walking tractors, a car, a seeding-machine and a harvester. The cultivated area of my family has reached 114 *mu* (7.6 hectares). Every year we sell over 20,000 kilograms of grain to the country, but we are not the best in Jiagen Village. One family plows 140 *mu* (9.3 hectares) of land!

V

"The old long-distance medical service of Tibet"

In 1966, Lhawang Duobujie started to work. He was a company commander of militia, secretary of the district party committee, vice-mayor of the county and vice-chairman of the county NPC standing committee. He was a good leader in Gyantse. After he went through retirement procedures, he was reemployed by the county government. He then worked at the county agricultural development office for many years. Now he is completely retired and lives his peaceful later years in Gyantse County.

I was born in Turugang Village of Gyantse County. My father was a serf of Qiangqin Monastery, in Rinpung. He ran away to Naro of Gyantse where he met my mother and married her. My mother escaped from the Kulong area of Rinpung where she had been a subject of Qudelin Monastery. Both of them became servants of a man called Tunbo in Gaxi Manor in Naro. Turugang Village had 42 families including 11 *tralpas*. The three families of Tunbo, Maiji and We were *tralpas*. Three *tralpa* families were self-contained and self-sufficient. And the remaining five *tralpas* were on the brink of bankruptcy. Apart from *tralpas*, 31 other families were tenants of small tracts of land that wasn't enough to guarantee the basic necessities.

A fertile land, Gaxi (meaning land of "four abundances" in Tibetan) used to be rich in "rivers, forests, grains and grass." Still serfs lived a hard life. My father died when I was eight years old, leaving three boys and one girl on a little plot of land. No matter how my mother worked for Tunbo, she couldn't support the whole family. My eldest brother went begging for food. My second brother died of hunger. When I was nine years old, my mother sent me to my aunt who lived in Rinpung. From 9 to 13, I helped them pasture sheep, feed cows, and fetch firewood. From 13 to 14, I worked in Qiangqin Monastery as a water fetcher. I had to wake up early in the morning and fetch water six times from a spring half a kilometer away.

Tibet's monasteries were just like the society. Some lamas were rich, some poor. Some big lamas lent money on usury with an interest of 125 percent and penalties for delay of payment. Some poor ones owed a lot of debts, so they had to become servants.

My aunt was too poor to support me and when I was 13 years old she sent me to a family named Talob. His family was rich. I pastured 200 sheep, six donkeys and three dzhos (cattle-yak crossbreed) for him. In the morning he would give me half a bowl of rough *tsamba* paste and another half at noon. I was always half hungry.

The old Tibet lagged behind in social development. There were no schools at all apart from private schools in big manors. Medical conditions were the same. There were few septuagenarians in the village. Patients were not able to see doctors. I heard of a doctor who lived near a village in a valley. If someone was sick in the village, the patient could put urine in a simple container and ask someone to climb the mountains to deliver the container to the doctor and ask for a prescription. As for the effectiveness of the prescriptions, nobody knew. I have heard that nowadays some hospitals rely on modern communications that enable them to give consultations remotely. Then this was far from the "telemedicine" or long-distance medical service of old Tibet!

Around the rebellion of 1959, there were many rumors. A lama said many of the Han died due to their offense against the local gods. Some armed rebel forces came later. They wore gold and silver decorations, saying that the Dalai Lama was bulletproof. The government clearly separated estate-holders into the patriotic ones and those who committed treason.

When I was 18, the democratic reform was launched in Tibet. Land was redistributed and my mother was given enough to live on. And so I was able to go home to my mother.

VI

"Democratic reform freed the serfs and me as well."

Horkhang Jampa Tenda has walked through smooth and bumpy roads in his life. In his later years, he takes the rough with the smooth. Since retirement, he travels to Jiama a dozen times every year, and he has made his contributions to the cultural development of his hometown. Though no one in Jiama is related to him, he has a lasting love and concern for his hometown. It is his unbreakable bond with the land.

Jiama Chikang was where my family lived in Medro Gongkar County. It used to be the hometown for 130,000 families. Then it became the manor of the Horkhang family. It has been there for more than 280 years. My family also had manors in Lhoka, Tabu, Chushul and Drigung. Of all the manors though, this was the main one since it was near Lhasa. All food and clothing was sent from here to Lhasa. Other manors also sent supplies every year, but they were

Jiama Chikang Manor in Medro Gongkar County

too far away from Lhasa. We sent the daily necessities, including *tsamba*, butter and meat to Lhasa.

My father, Horkhang Tasa Sodnams Palvbar, didn't join the rebellion in 1959. He was appointed an official of Chamdo in 1947 and lived there from 1947 to 1950. He returned home in 1951 after Chamdo was liberated. An official of the fourth rank in the local government, he was promoted to the third rank, Tasa, when he went to Lhasa. He became a commissioner of Chamdo. Later, in 1959, he returned to Lhasa and assumed the office of director of teaching in the Tibetan Cadres' School, teaching the Tibetan language.

After the democratic reform in 1959, the country paid us according to a certain proportion of cultivated land, houses, means of production and livestock and then distributed these to the people. We had houses in Lhasa. Our servants went back to their own homes. They all got cultivated land. Since

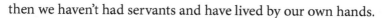

then we haven't had servants and have lived by our own hands.

Later my father worked in the Counselors' Office of the Autonomous Region. I was 15 years old during the democratic reform. In the beginning, for two years, there were no changes to the pasturing industry. There was a policy binding herdsmen and herd owners.

During the democratic reform, our properties remained intact as we didn't participate in the rebellion. Now my father was called home for discussions about how to handle the matter of his property because there was a new land policy. My father said that, except for some Tibetan classic books, everything was to be given to the people. He didn't want anything. At that time he came from Lhasa in a carriage. When he went back, he carried nothing but some Buddhist scriptures because my father attached great importance to Tibetan culture. Everything else was distributed to the people.

Padrup, a 78-year-old former private school teacher of Chikang Village, interrupted: "At that time there were few educated people in rural areas, so we were popular. I remember we were the ones who read government policies at meetings. The people hailed the democratic reform. After the reform, there were no corvees, no debts that drove people to exile. Instead, they were given cultivated land per capita. Some areas were large, so a person could be given four *mu* of land. Some areas were small, but still people might get three *mu*.

"The government collected all the means of production then distributed them to people in need. It was the same procedure for livestock. Those belonging to Chikang Manor remained there. The stock belonging to Tabarazhang Manor remained with that manor as well. The rest was given to nine herdsmen. Some poor families were given livestock. So all of us were happy. Those without land now had cultivated land; those working without payment now could enjoy the fruit of their own labor."

After the rebellion, some officials of local government ran away with the Dalai Lama to India. Others showed support for the Central People's

Government. Ngapoi is a relative to my family. On the day before the rebellion, he sent a car to pick us up, but we did not want to be involved in the rebellion.

After the suppression of the rebellion, my father served as a member, a standing member, and vice-chairman of People's Political Consultative Conference of Tibet Autonomous Region. He remained busy until his death. He was a well-known scholar in Tibet. Influenced by him, I worked hard for cultural development and cultural relics protection in Jiama. I was a member of the autonomous region's conference. My father placed great importance on culture. He set up a private school, and taught Tibetan, calligraphy, arithmetic, and more. He enrolled over 30 students, including children from rich families and orphans. After the democratic reform, they became teachers or drivers. During the People's Communes movement, many of the accountants and reporters were students of these private schools.

A scenery in today's Jiama

With democratic reform, we sent away all our servants. None of them remained. Most of them came from Jiama. Before that, we were nobles. We hadn't worked and we didn't know how to work. Cooking or fetching water, all was done by servants. I was little, did not know how to tie my shoes. I didn't know how to put on clothes. I remember that when my mother first made steamed bread, she failed and the steamed bread was turned to dough. It was very difficult in the beginning, but gradually we learned to do housework, and later we could manage all the chores.

After graduation from the university, I was assigned to Chamdo region and came back to Lhasa several years later. I heard that after the Cultural Revolution, our house at the Grand Mosque in the old downtown of Lhasa was returned to us. However, the 10,000-square-meter house was full of people who had nowhere to go. My father then decided not to reclaim the house and applied for another place to build a new house.

Since my retirement, I come to Jiama every year, as there is a bond between us. They (referring to Teacher Padrup and others) were freed after the democratic reform. So was I. If I was in the old society, I would have much to worry about: taxes for local government, management of people in the manor. That would be a headache! Now I live a comfortable life without worries. Isn't that good?

We were good playmates in childhood and we still are good friends, indicating an old man of the village. At that time his father was a servant of the manor. He was 12 and I was 10. Now we are very good friends and visit each other often. The democratic reform freed those poor people as well as such nobles as myself. We respect each other, help each other and live in a harmonious society. Why should we live a society that lacks harmony?

My Miserable Family

Narrator: Makar
Recorder: Yang Feng

My home is in the Ruli grasslands of Nakchu in Tibet. There are majestic snow-capped mountains, bubbling hot springs, limpid rivers, green grassland, and herds of sheep and cattle covering the land. What an abundant land it is! But, before the democratic reform in 1959, all of this wealth was in the hands of three major estate-holders, namely, the Kasha (the former local government of Tibet), noblemen and upper-ranking lamas in the monasteries. The rest, the majority, lived a miserable life of poverty.

Take my family for instance! My grandfather was a *trapla*. He had some sheep and cattle and a certain degree of freedom. Through the industrious work of my grandfather, father and mother, we could make a living. But this life did not last long.

For no reason, their serf-owner, Tsering Langpei, took away our sheep and cattle. There was no system of justice and the family went broke. My grandfather died of rage.

Tsering Langpei continued to harass us. One day, he took some men to my home, and said to my father, "Your father owe me a debt. You have to pay it back today!"

My father replied with constrained anger, "I don't know about my father's debt to you. But it's clear that you have taken away all our sheep and cattle, so I have nothing left to give you."

The serf-owner said resentfully, "If you can't repay me, then we shall meet with the Kasha! Your debt was for them."

This was just a lame excuse. While he was saying this, he had his men tie my father onto a horse and lead him away. My mother went up to help my father, but was knocked down.

Watching all this, we children cried loudly. My mother struggled to get up from the ground. Suddenly she picked up my youngest brother and rushed to the house of the serf-owner. The rest of us followed her.

When we got to the house, we saw father tied down and placed on a stone stele, with a huge rock on his back. We felt as if a knife were being twisted in our hearts.

Tsering Langpei laughed ferociously: "Ha Ha! You've all come. That saves my invitation. Have a look at how I punish a debtor!" He held a big club as he was saying this and beat my dad. There was blood and torn pieces of flesh all around. Mother fainted and we cried.

When he stopped, we opened our eyes and saw two white bones pointing out from father's body. The flesh and blood was splashed on the ground and walls. How horrible it was!

But Tsering Langpei still wouldn't release my father. He shut my father in a dark and damp dungeon, where my father's injury got worse. After a few days, he died miserably.

Under the feudal serfdom system, serfs could be tortured by the serf-owners as they saw fit. Even a disobedient word would lead to harsh punishment.

Mother said, "My husband has been beaten to death. How can these children live?" The serf-owner then accused her of "being against the Heaven's will" and "Buddha's punishment." He took her and beat her too, leaving severe wounds on her belly. The wounds later became inflamed and gathered flies. My poor mother, just like my father, died miserably at the hands of the serf-owner.

My parents died leaving nine orphans ranging from one to thirteen. How could we survive? Today orphans are not only adopted by the government, but also go to school when they come of school age. But at that time, orphans would only starve to death.

My heart broke when I saw my younger sisters' and brothers' big eyes eager for food and heard their pitiful cries: "Sister, I am hungry! I want something to eat!" My tears burst out like water in a river!

I am the fourth child. My two elder sisters, an elder brother and I searched the grassland for some dead animals and dragged them home for food. Once we found a little calf. We dragged it home, skinned it, cut meat from the leg and started a fire. We stewed the meat in a pot. Smelling the sweet aroma and waiting to taste the delicious beef, my younger brothers and sisters were overjoyed and started to sing and dance. It was a rare happy moment for us.

Suddenly Tsering Langpei came out of nowhere.

Seeing us cooking the meat, he said coldly, "The dead cattle and sheep on the grassland are my tribute to the Divine Bird; any cow dung on the grassland is my property. How dare you take them away from me?"

He then kicked the pot over. The boiling water burned my younger brothers and sisters. Looking at the fierce and malicious Tsering Langpei, I hated him. How I wish I could stab him to death.

He left. We picked up the beef. But we dared not cook it, so we cut the meat into small pieces to feed my brothers and sisters. But their immature stomachs couldn't digest the raw meat. My two younger sisters died soon after they ate it. So we did not give any to our younger brothers, but dug wild vegetables for them.

These little boys could not survive on wild vegetables and soon they died of hunger as well. How lovely if there was a place in the world in which the poor wouldn't get harmed or be hungry!

My Life as a Serf

After my four younger brothers and sisters died, all five of us, seven and above, were forced by Tsering Langpei to become the serfs of his sons. He ordered us not to speak, meet or communicate with each other. I was sent to Dormgje, a far more atrocious and hellish man than his father. He killed people for no reason.

On the first day I walked into the house of Dormgje, he asked me directly, "Do you remember how your parents died?"

As a little girl, I didn't understand the meaning behind the question, so I

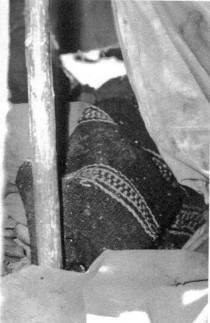

A dying serf in a shabby tent

replied honestly: "Yes."

He grunted: "Yes? That's good! If you disobey my orders, you will die like your parents. Am I understood?"

I stared at his ugly face and said nothing.

He shouted to the house and a kind-looking elder sister came out.

He ordered, "Take her to the doghouse." The girl waved to me and I followed her out of the courtyard.

"How did you get here?" she whispered to me and continued without my answer. "Wait and see. It is just the beginning of hell!" Her tears dropped when she said these.

The doghouse was a dirty and smelly shed built of cobblestone. It was not suitable for a dog, let alone a human being. I looked at the doghouse, stupefied.

The girl read my mind and said to me with tears: "You clean it first. Later I will bring you a felt."

She added, "My name is Pekyi. Come to me if you have trouble in the future. I should go back now or I will be punished."

I looked around the doghouse and saw wooden stakes for fastening cattle and sheep were all around. My job then was to pasture cattle and sheep on the grassland during the day and keep them in the doghouse at night.

When I was 10, the ewes gave birth to many lambs in the spring. One day I found a lamb was missing. The next day, Dormgje found it was eaten by wolves. At dusk when I returned, he called me, caught my braids, took out his knife and cut a piece of flesh out of my right thigh.

He picked up the flesh on the point and said with teeth clenched: "You fed my lamb to the wolves and I will feed you your own flesh. Take a bite! How does it taste?" He said and stuffed the flesh into my mouth.

I passed out on the spot. I lay on the ground, bleeding. But Dormgje went away, as if nothing had happened. Pekyi heard the noise and rushed to me and took me to the doghouse. She placed dried cow dung on my wound to stop the bleeding. I clung tightly to her, while she held me sadly.

We said not a word. What could we say? To whom could we tell our stories? What changes would be made? We both stayed silent for a while, and she went away with tears on her face.

Under Pekyi's care, I got better and was able to do some light work. Dormgje said: "You have enough rest! Go and pasture my calves. I don't feed a useless person!"

Dormgje put a dozen calves under my care and called another male serf, Dhondup, to help to pasture the cows. From then on, I had to limp to the mountain to pasture them. To prevent the calves from nursing, the cows and calves were separated into two pastures. We still had to keep the calves from running to the cows and this was exhausting work everyday.

One day, it rained hailstones. The animals got mixed together. As a result, some calves were able to nurse. It wasn't such a big problem since the calves and cows were all his. But Dormgje scolded us. He picked up a rock, chased after Dhondup and blinded his left eye. Then he came to me, took out the sword and cut me in the left knee. The serf-owner treasured the little milk of the cow but left us bleeding on the ground.

I cried and passed out. Pekyi heard it and once again took me to the doghouse. In those days, every time we met, we cried. When would such tribulations end?

I couldn't go pasturing, so Dormgje told me to look after the drying butter. I should be alert all the time and keep the crows and domesticated animals away. The vats of butters were widely placed on the ground, without any fences. I had injuries so it was hard for me to take care of the butter. A wild billy goat intruded and ate some butter. My friend Matsomo helped me chase it away. Dormgje's wife saw it all and took out a knife and rushed after me. I knew I would suffer misfortune again and I called Matsomo for help. Matsomo was about my age and very much afraid of Dormgje's wife. She was scared and ran away at once!

Then the mean woman caught me. Knowing I had wounds on both of my legs she cut me on the left wrist. This way I could continue pasturing for her but she could vent her anger on me.

The troubled days continued and my hatred grew. One spring, a mare gave birth to a foal. Dormgje's younger brother Caiwang Rigzin came to see it. He was about my age. He did nothing but played all day and wore beautiful clothes. I had neither food nor clothes, but I had to do all the dirty and heavy work.

When I saw such a contrast I was deeply discontented and couldn't help complaining before him.

I said: "I have no food, no clothes, but have to do all the pasturing and I am even tortured. How can I live such a life?" Unfortunately Caiwang Rigzin went back and repeated my words to Dormgje.

Dormgje came and scolded me: "You still owe me a debt, but I adopted you. Instead of being appreciative, you are dissatisfied." He took a club and beat me hard. I bled at the mouth, ears and nose. At night, I suffered from so much swelling.

Pekyi brought me some alkaline soil, and cried: "I cannot come visiting you often, as I have a lot of work to do. If you feel painful, put some of this in water and drink it." With her care, I suddenly felt better. I used the "medicine" to ease the pain. Today when the weather changes, I still feel the pain all over, that's the effect of a hard beating.

Would I see the end of it? After such an injury, I couldn't go pasturing during the day, but I had to look after the livestock in the shabby doghouse at night.

One stormy night, the sheep and cattle got scared and took off. Due to my severe injury, I couldn't chase after them. When the rain stopped, other serfs brought them back. I should not have been blamed since all the sheep and cattle were back.

But I had an ominous presentiment. When I lay down on bed, I smelled misfortune for the next day. I spent a sleepless night. I was thinking: if I were an eagle, I could fly away; if I were a mouse, I could hide away; if I were a fish, I could swim away…but I am just a child with injuries all over my body, waiting to be tortured!

Early next morning, Dormgje came to my door and shouted: "Makar, come out!"

Hearing his voice, I was scared to death. With wounds all over, I walked to the door. He leapt forward, dragged me out and knocked me down. He stepped on my neck, and drew out the sword. He cut me twice on my calf and gave me another stab on my left instep.

My miserable cries broke the silence of the dawn. My only friend Pekyi woke up from dreams and rushed to the doghouse in a hurry. At the sight of Dormgje torturing me and seeing me covered in blood, she just broke down.

Dear Pekyi, what could you do about it when you came? The same disaster might fall on you! Dormgje was still there so Pekyi wouldn't dare come to me. She could do nothing but turn back. Three knife scars were added to my body!

I became an adult of 18. One day, I was washing my hair beside the Luohe River, and saw my face in the river and grew sad suddenly! I had the same numbers of nose and eyes as the serf-owner had. Why should I be tortured by him? I am a human being, so is he. Why should I be humble before him and he be a bully before me? I grew more and more desperate! It would be better if I jumped into the Luohe River!

When I was thinking this, Pekyi came to fetch water. She called me when she saw me staring at the river. I came back from deep thought. I was surprised to find that I had been thinking of death. I cried in her arms. She held me tight and touched my head.

Her voice was so kind: "Don't cry, my sister, there's no use crying…"

Though she said so, I couldn't help it.

I couldn't take it any longer, so I decided to escape. I looked for an opportunity to escape. When I heard that Dormgje would go out the next day, I decided to run. I prepared everything that night and waited him to leave in the morning.

The next morning, he rode away. I picked up my stuff and ran away along the lower reaches of the Luohe River. But, it was a vast grassland. He found me and chased me on his horse. I felt so anxious that I jumped into the Luohe River.

I was recaptured. He asked his wife and brother to hold me down. They grasped my hands and he drew out a knife, saying: "Never think you are old enough to fly away. I will chop your feet off if you flee again!"

He cut down and I felt a hell of pain on my right ankle. I passed out. When I woke up, I found myself lying in the doghouse. Pekyi was beside me in tears.

"My foot?"

I pulled up my body in a panic.

"It is all right, it is going to get better. I have bound it up." Pekyi comforted me and asked me to rest.

In 10 years, I was cut seven times by Dormgje.

He said shamelessly in public, "I cut you seven times and you still live. You must have nine lives. It's Buddha who blesses you!"

Young people today might hardly imagine how a person could kill a human as if he would slaughter a sheep. But this was indeed the fate of serfs under the feudal serfdom system in Tibet. The scars on my body are the evidence. The Dalai Lama faction wanted to restore such a system. They speak of "human rights" but what about the human rights of serfs like me?

Hope Dawns

In the winter of 1951, a piece of exciting news spread on the grassland: the Red Hans were in Lhasa. The Red Hans!

Everyone wanted to know what they were like.

Pilgrims from Lhasa said, "The Hans have red lights on their heads (the red five-pointed stars on the cap). They have smiles on their faces."

Tradesmen selling hides came back and said, "The Hans don't take things from people, they purchase everything using silver dollars."

Travelling artists said, "The Hans and Tibetans are friends. They are giving candies to children and *tsamba* to adults."

But Dormgje said, "I know that the Hans capture children and cook them for food. They also kill adults."

I thought that the Hans could not be worse than Dormgje. On a night with the bright moon and few stars, Pekyi came to the doghouse, whispering in my ears.

"I heard Dormgje was telling his wife that the Hans are enemies of the rich but friends of the poor. If the Hans come, it will not be good for the rich people, but the poor will have a lot of benefits!" she said.

I hugged Pekyi and said with excitement, "If it is true, our bitter

An abundant grassland

days are about to end."

We looked forward to the appearance of the Hans day and night, and looked for the Hans with the red lights on their heads. The wait was killing us!

Then one day at noon, I was pasturing at the foot of Pargalalong Mountain. Suddenly a young lady came out of nowhere. She looked familiar, but I didn't recognize her. She came over to me and sat down beside me. She took out two pancakes, one for her and one for me. I took the cake and looked at her carefully, wondering why a strange sister gave me something to eat.

She saw my face and smiled: "Take a bite."

After having the pancake, she spoke to me and asked what my name was, who my master was, and who else was in my family. When it came to my family, I couldn't help crying. She was very sympathetic to me, and told me not to be sad and to tell her everything.

Having led a miserable life under Dormgje's rule, I told her everything. So I told her about my family and my sufferings. Her tears burst out when she listened. She looked even sadder than I did.

I asked: "Sister, do you suffer the same pain as I do?"

She wept off her tears and said happily: "I am your sister Danzhu!"

We hugged each other hard and cried out loud. Oh, she is my own sister! We sisters had been separated by the serf-owner for more than a decade. I didn't expect that we would have ever met again!

I listened and was enthralled at stories my sister told about the Hans. Sister said: "I've come all this way to find you. We will run away together!"

I had no confidence since I was recaptured last time.

"Where shall we run?" I said doubtfully.

"To places where there are Hans!"

"What if Dormgje chases us?"

"We don't need to be afraid of him, we have the Hans (to help us)."

These words reminded me that recently Dormgje seemed to be less vicious. He dared not hurt people like he used to do. I thought my sister was right and decided to escape with her.

I left Dormgje's sheep and cattle and ran to Pargalalong Mountain with my sister. Halfway up the mountain, a man stopped us.

Just when I was about to defend myself, the man asked with a smile: "Is this Sister Makar? I am your brother-in-law."

Sister said hastily: "He waits for us." I let out my breath in a long sigh. I was so lucky to have escaped the hell at last.

We walked southwards for seven days and reached Santa in the Kongpo area. We met the Hans in army uniform there. Really, each of them has a star giving off a red light on their heads.

My brother-in-law told me: "They are Hans, People's Liberation Army (PLA) soldiers."

I met the PLA soldiers. I was too happy to say a word. Warmth came out of my chest and I couldn't help bursting into tears. The PLA soldiers saw us and asked us to have a rest. They invited us to tea, and asked us where we came from and where we wanted to go. Though we didn't understand their language, we could tell from their expressions and gestures. I answered in Tibetan. They gave us a plate of rice and two plates of food.

Two soldiers saw that my sister and I didn't wear shoes, and then gave us a pair each. Before we left, they gave us another packet of rice, and said a lot to us that we didn't understand. I recalled thinking that they must be from Heaven.

We met the PLA soldiers and felt hope was within our reach. We decided to go to Midika, the hometown of my brother-in-law, and waited for the PLA soldiers to go there.

I firmly believed that Hans are good people! The PLA soldiers are good people! How I wish they would come to northern Tibet with us, to Midika, to clear away devils like Dormgje.

We settled down in Midika, living as blacksmiths. Although life was still very hard, I had much more freedom and happiness than being a serf in the house of a serf-owner.

In March 1959, the Dalai Lama faction launched an armed rebellion in Lhasa and Lhoka. The PLA soldiers suppressed the rebellion. The rebellion in Lhasa was over within two weeks.

One day, the rebellious army rushed into Midika. Seeing their discomposure, we saw that they had suffered a recent defeat. The next day, they ran away but the PLA soldiers caught up with them.

After the rebellion was suppressed, local governments sent work teams to establish herdsman committees on the grassland. This is how the move towards democratic reform began. The herdsmen, used to be those being trampled upon, were given sheep and cattle and allowed to establish homes.

The liberated herdsmen were singing and dancing on the vast grassland to celebrate. The PLA soldiers had helped us shake off our chains and led us to a new life.

My New Life

After the democratic reform, the good news continued. In 1961, a chemical factory was erected on the grasslands of Nakchu, and herdsmen were invited to work there. Some herdsmen and I applied for the jobs.

In the factory we were given butter, *tsamba* and tea to eat and lived in new tents. We worked hard but we were not forced to do this. We received good treatment. We had just been freed from the feudal serfdom system and so it still felt a little peculiar.

For the first time, I felt happy to work; for the first time, I was taken care of by many people; and I became a human being with dignity. My heart was filled with honey and I worked like a hot iron!

I worked about a month in the factory and then one day the team leader asked me to take my salary. I thought that meals were enough pay for me. What was a salary for? I didn't know so I didn't go.

Afterwards the team leader urged me: "Makar, go and get your salary. You are making the accountant wait for you!"

The first generation of Tibetan women workers

I saw the leader meant it so I went to the office and was given 76 silver dollars. I couldn't believe my eyes. It was more than all my father could earn and save. I was so surprised. I asked how many years the salary was for. They told me that it was just for a month. I still could not believe my ears and I asked the accountant, who again confirmed it.

I hurried to fetch my apron into which 76 silver dollars were poured, heavy and hard. I couldn't believe that it was my own money.

I used the money to buy clothes, quilt, bed sheet, basin, towel, toothbrush and other utensils. And there was still plenty left. I took my purchases back to the tent and had a look at them one after another.

All the past came to mind. I burst into tears. I couldn't help but kneel down in front of the picture of Chairman Mao. Staring at his kind face, I cried in my heart: "Long Live Chairman Mao!"

Not long after I was elected as production leader. I never thought that I could have such a bright life. I expected a humble life, but I got so much more that I couldn't believe it. After working for a year in the chemical plant, I was transferred to Lhasa Nagin Electric Power Plant. I knew that electric power plant gave us light. I decided that I would work my best to help illuminate Lhasa forever.

On the National Day of 1964, I was invited to Beijing for the celebrations of the 15th anniversary of the founding of New China. I was granted an audience with Chairman Mao. It was the biggest honor of my life.

Looking back on my entire life, I suffered from brutal torture under the feudal serfdom system during the first 20 years, but I enjoyed warmth and happiness, as well as dignity and honor, in the second half of my life.

What is a good society and what is a bad one? I have found my own answer. The Dalai Lama faction vainly attempted to separate Tibet from China. It was nothing but wishful thinking. It is nothing but their particular daydream!

图书在版编目（CIP）数据

生活在世界屋脊上：英文 / 金志国主编. -- 北京：
新世界出版社，2010.11
ISBN 978-7-5104-1414-5

Ⅰ.①生… Ⅱ.①金… Ⅲ.①纪实文学－中国－当代－英文 Ⅳ.①I25
中国版本图书馆CIP数据核字（2010）第222593号

生活在世界屋脊上（英）

主　　编：金志国
策　　划：张海鸥　李淑娟
责任编辑：李淑娟
翻　　译：传神联合（北京）信息技术有限公司
英文改稿：Stephanie Buzzarte Tansey, David A. Peck
英文审定：姜竹青
图片提供：《中国西藏》杂志　格勒　羽芊　金勇　中国日报社
装帧设计：青青虫工作室
责任印制：李一鸣　黄厚清
出版发行：新世界出版社
社　　址：北京市西城区百万庄大街24号（100037）
总编室电话：＋86 10 6899 5424　　68326679（传真）
发行部电话：＋86 10 6899 5968　　68998705（传真）
本社中文网址：http://www.nwp.cn
本社英文网址：http://www.newworld-press.com
版权部电子信箱：frank@nwp.com.cn
版权部电话：＋86 10 6899 6306
印刷：北京京华虎彩印刷有限公司
经销：新华书店
开本：787 × 1092　　1/16
字数：200千字　　　印张：15.25
版次：2011年1月第1版　2011年1月北京第1次印刷
书号：ISBN 978-7-5104-1414-5
定价：78.00元